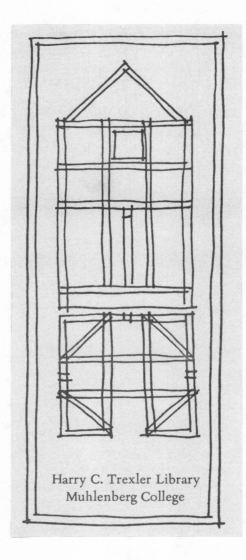

International Trade and Economic Development

Gottfried Haberler

International Center
for Economic Growth

Affiliated with the
Institute for Contemporary Studies

International Trade and Economic Development

Inquiries, book orders, and catalog requests should be addressed
to International Center for Economic Growth, 243 Kearney St.,
San Francisco, CA 94108. Telephone: (415) 981-5353

ISBN: 1-55815-022-6

CONTENTS

PREFACE

This monograph, by Gottfried Haberler, is the first in the Center's Reprint Series. The series will reissue out of print or limited edition articles or books of significant merit for policy makers, thus refocusing attention on important development issues and their policy implications.

We are extremely pleased to inaugurate this new series with lectures by Gottfried Haberler. In his career of more than half a century, he has made important contributions advancing the discipline of economics, especially in international trade and development. His work in the areas of comparative advantage and the welfare implications of free trade and protection has had a major influence on trade policy, and in turn has affected the course of development economics. He has thus contributed to the advancement of economic theory and the improvement of policy formulation. He has been widely recognized by the economics profession with honors such as the Presidency of the American Economic Association in 1963.

The lectures are presented by an introduction, written for this publication, that clarifies certain issues of import to Professor Haberler. Spanning over thirty years, the lectures—the Cairo lectures of 1959 and the 1987 Pioneers lecture with comments by W. Max Corden and Ronald Findlay—demonstrate the timeless nature of Professor Haberler's analysis and policy recommendations. We are confident that these recommendations remain valuable for both economists and policymakers.

Nicolás Ardito-Barletta
General Director
International Center
  for Economic Growth

Panama City, Panama
July, 1988

ABOUT THE AUTHOR

Gottfried Haberler is Galen L. Stone Professor of International Trade, emeritus, Harvard University. Over the course of his career, he has made outstanding contributions in the field of economics, through his work in such areas as international trade, terms of trade, and foreign exchange. Professor Haberler is a former president (1950–51) and honorary president (since 1953) of the International Economic Association, former president of the National Bureau of Economic Research (1955), and former president of the American Economic Association (1963). He has been awarded honorary degrees from several European universities. Among his many publications are his classic work *The Theory of International Trade, with its Application to Commercial Policy* (1936), *Prosperity and Depression* (1937), and *Selected Essays of Gottfried Haberler* (1985). Professor Haberler is currently a resident scholar at the American Enterprise Institute, in Washington, DC.

Introduction

More than thirty years have elapsed since I first wrote on economic development. More than a half century has passed since my first published paper on international trade and trade policy,[1] and a quarter century lies between the lectures reprinted in this volume.[2]

Much has changed during this time. The general posture of economic policy in many countries has changed. Our perceptions of the past have shifted. Methods of theoretical analysis have been refined—often to the point of zero marginal returns—and torrents of statistical data, often of questionable value, have surged from national governments and international agencies.

I must confess that despite all these changes, I still maintain my early beliefs in the validity of classical or neoclassical theory[3] and the superiority of liberal economic policies—defining the term "economic liberalism" in the original, classical sense of relying largely on competitive markets and private enterprise. I do realize however, that by making unrealistic assumptions about inelasticities, rigidities, externalities, and the alleged irrational behavior of market participants, especially lowly farmers in less developed countries (LDCs), it is possible to use the tools of neoclassical trade theory for developing logically valid arguments for pernicious interventionist and protectionist policies.

The Decline and Resurgence of Economic Liberalism

In my *Pioneers* lecture I noted that after World War II, when the problem of growth and development in the Third World was thrust upon the West by the breakup of the colonial empires, faith in capitalism and free markets was at an all-time low, especially among economists and intellectuals. I mentioned two reasons for the low level of confidence. First, the legacy of the Great Depression of the 1930s which was misinterpreted both by Marxists and by Keynes and his numerous followers as being due to a basic flaw in capitalism. Second, the apparent immunity of Stalin's Russia to the catastrophic depression that engulfed the West and the great early economic successes of Hitler's Germany strongly affected the West and persuaded many of Keynes' followers of the superiority of central planning over private enterprise and free markets. The lack of faith in the efficacy of the price mechanism was strikingly illustrated by the popularity of the theory of the permanent dollar shortage which was embraced not only by some radical followers of Keynes, such as Thomas (Lord) Balogh and Joan Robinson, but also by *The Economist*, and in a more sophisticated form by two extremely influential economists, J. R. Hicks and D. H. Robertson. In view of all this, it is not surprising that economic policy in most Third World countries has been, and in many countries still is, anything but liberal in the classical sense.

In the Western democracies, the demise of economic liberalism did not last long. In Western Europe the change came dramatically in 1948 with the famous currency and economic reform in Germany. The large monetary overhang inherited from the war was slashed, and the tight web of price and wage controls and consumer rationing that prevented the huge stock of money from driving up prices was abolished overnight. Many economists, especially followers of Keynes such as Balogh and J. K. Galbraith, predicted dire consequences: the lifting of controls would create chaos, and the

Soviet Zone of Germany would outproduce the West. In fact, the opposite occurred. The German economic minister Ludwig Erhard's bold step ushered in the German economic miracle, which gave a powerful boost to the economies of other countries in Europe and beyond and inspired similar reforms in France, Italy, and Austria. There has been some backsliding in a few countries, but by and large economic liberalism has progressed in the Western world. More recently, the elections of Ronald Reagan and Margaret Thatcher have given liberalism a strong push.

Today, the contrast between free market and centrally planned economies has become so glaring that it can no longer be overlooked. Compare, for example, the situations in West and East Germany; Austria and Czechoslovakia; Taiwan and mainland China; and South and North Korea. Indeed, some socialist or labor party governments in the West, Spain, Australia, New Zealand have started to liberalize. Even some communist countries, notably Hungary and to a lesser extent Poland, are trying with some success to raise productivity and output by giving market forces some scope. Hungary has outperformed its hard-line communist neighbors, Czechoslovakia and Romania. Under Mikhail Gorbachev in Soviet Russia itself, the inefficiency and wastefulness of tightly centralized planning are aired in public. This has been highlighted by the fact that shabbiness and poor quality have made the exportation of Soviet nondefense manufactured products to countries outside the Soviet sphere, and even to Soviet satellite countries, almost impossible.

The Diversity of the Third World

It is not easy to determine whether there has been a pronounced trend toward the liberalization of economic policy in the Third World. The "developing" countries, as they are officially called, are a very heterogeneous group.

In my Cairo lectures, I have argued at some length that the widely accepted procedure of taking per capita real income as a measure of the level of development is, strictly speaking, not quite satisfactory. We can imagine a country with a poorly educated people sitting on a pool of oil enjoying a high per capita income. We might also imagine a country with a highly educated people so poorly endowed with natural resources and bad climate that the per capita income is comparatively low.

Fortunately, in practice we need not take such conceptual difficulties very seriously. This is suggested by a statement of Herman Weyl, the outstanding mathematician and philosopher of science. In his celebrated book *Philosophy of Mathematics and the Natural Science*, he wrote that it often happens in scientific pursuits "that the typical may be elusive in terms of well-defined concepts and yet we handle it with instinctive certitude, e.g., in recognizing persons." Surely, what is good enough for the "hard" natural sciences should satisfy us in the social sciences. I conclude that it would be a mistake to quibble about a precise definition. Instead, I accept the widely used distinction between the rich North of the industrial countries versus the poor South of the less developed or developing countries—South minus Australia, New Zealand and South Africa.

The great diversity of the Third World is a fact of utmost importance. There are, at one end of the spectrum, the so-called NICs, newly industrializing countries, Taiwan, South Korea, Hong Kong, Singapore—countries well on their way to joining the club of developed industrial countries. There can be little doubt that these countries owe their success largely to the relatively liberal policies—liberal, that is, compared to those of many LDCs. In my *Pioneers* lecture I gave the economic liberalism of the "gang of four" too high a mark; I accept Ronald Findlay's criticism on that point. Only Hong Kong can be said to practice a policy close to laissez faire. Still, as Findlay says, "state intervention in these economies has a complementary rather than restrictive or tutelary relationship to the private sector, as in India, for example." These governments make full use of private entrepreneurial talents and avoid high inflation and stifling controls.

At the other end of the spectrum are very poor countries like Bangladesh and much of Africa, often called the "Fourth World." Between the two extremes are the oil-producing countries, which are usually treated as a group, as distinguished from the non-oil-producing LDCs. But the dividing line between the two poles is somewhat arbitrary and the non-oil- producing countries are also a very heterogeneous group. Finally, there are the Latin American countries, sometimes called the middle-income countries, frequently characterized by overindebtedness and inflation.

The great diversity of the Third World countries makes it difficult to determine firmly and precisely whether a pronounced trend toward liberalization has occurred there as in the developed countries. But let me be bold and give my general impression. I do not think that there so far has been a general change in economic policy, but I do have the impression that there is growing awareness that there is something wrong with both the development policy pursued by most LDCs since World War II and the underlying theory. Furthermore, expert opinion in the developed countries and in most international agencies on problems of development in the LDCs has changed with the resurgence of liberalism described above.

The Impact of Foreign Trade and Investment on Third World Countries

Experience of the past thirty years or so has clearly shown that development policies that pay little or no attention to the vital contribution of foreign trade, private enterprise and direct foreign investment, do not yield sustained and efficient industrialization and growth. On the contrary, the result has been indiscriminate protection, grossly inefficient subsidized private and government-operated enterprise and corrosive inflation.

The change in outlook away from these policies that has taken place is highlighted by the World Bank's *World Development Report 1987*[4] which stresses the vital contribution of foreign trade for achieving rapid development. This report draws attention to the views presented by John Stuart Mill in his *Principles of Political Economy* (1st edition 1848) regarding the impact of foreign trade on the development of poor countries.

As I have discussed in the *Pioneers* lecture, Mill distinguished between direct and indirect effects. The direct—or static—effect results from the division of labor according to comparative cost. The indirect—or dynamic—effect, which Mill believed to have the greater impact, is created by placing people in contact with "persons dissimilar to themselves," where they are exposed to new "modes of thought." Mill concludes that the effects of foreign trade are greatest on countries in the early stages of industrialization.

But perhaps the best historical defense of foreign trade comes from most unlikely sources. One hundred and forty years ago, Karl Marx and Friedrich Engels in their famous *Communist Manifesto* (1848) presented a glowing description of the power of free trade to spur the development of LDCs. I quote what Joseph A. Schumpeter has to say about the *Communist Manifesto*.

> Never and in particular by no modern defender of the bourgeois civilization has anything like this been penned, never has a brief been composed on behalf of the business class from so profound and so wide a comprehension of what its achievement is and of what it means to humanity.[5]

It should be kept in mind that Marx's 19th century terminology differs from the present one. What we now call capitalism, he called the "bourgeoisie." What we call less-developed or poor countries, he called "the barbarians." The *Communist Manifesto* should be required reading for self-styled Marxist leaders of developing countries.

Development Economics: A Critical Analysis

The theory behind the policy of rapid government-sponsored industrialization with limited foreign trade—a policy that unfortunately is still pursued by many developing countries—reflects the demise of liberalism and the widespread belief in the superiority of central planning over free markets and private enterprise in the early post-World War II period. Specifically, it was the consequence of the misinterpretation by Keynes and his followers of the Great Depression of the 1930s as due to a basic flaw in capitalism.

Keynes' faulty vision was eagerly accepted in the Third World. This was well illustrated by the work of the late Raul Prebisch, one of the most influential theorists and practitioners of economic development. Prebisch related that, like Keynes, in the 1920s he "was a firm believer in the neoclassical theories." But "the first great crisis of capitalism," the world depression of the 1930s, changed his mind. While Keynes later found his way back to his early classical beliefs, Prebisch did not. He reported that, "The second great crisis of capitalism, which we are all suffering now, has strengthened my attitude." That second great crisis, according to Prebisch, was the world recession of the early 1980s. To call it "a great crisis of capitalism," resembling the Great Depression of the 1930s, is a grotesque misinterpretation. Compared with the depression of the 1930s, it was a mild recession caused by the Federal Reserve and some other central banks stepping on the monetary brake to bring down a two-digit inflation. Some monetarists and supply-siders—odd bedfellows—have argued that the recession could have been avoided if the monetary brake had been applied more gently. I doubt it, but whatever the answer, it does not change the nature of the actual outcome: a comparatively mild recession, and certainly not a crisis of capitalism.

The Deterioration of the Terms of Trade of the LDCs

I now discuss three important theories which assert that foreign trade often has a negative effect on the economies of the LDCs. The most important one probably is the Prebisch-Singer theory of secular deterioration of the LDCs' terms of trade; it asserts that the prices of the LDCs' main exports, raw materials and foodstuffs— primary products for short—have a pronounced secular tendency to decline in relation to the prices of manufactured goods. This theory is largely the consequence of the misinterpretation of the Great Depression of the 1930s. It is true that during the depression commodity prices declined much more sharply than prices of manufactures. But later research has definitely shown that this was a cyclical decline, and that there has been no secular deterioration.[8]

Prices of primary products exhibit, as a rule, sharper cyclical fluctuations than prices of manufactured products. That implies that the terms of trade of LDCs deteriorate in recessions. But it does not imply that the LDCs, the "periphery" in Prebisch's terminology, suffer more in recessions than the industrial centers; the

LDCs suffer from a deterioration of their terms of trade—the industrial countries from unemployment. I leave open the question of which is more painful.

A real grievance of the LDCs is protectionism—especially agricultural protectionism—in the industrial countries. Sugar is a shocking example. U.S. import restrictions keep the price of sugar at about five times the world market level, implying an enormous misallocation of productive resources. And for two reasons this policy even has an adverse effect on U.S. national security. It locks Cuba more firmly into the Soviet orbit because the Soviet Union buys a large part of the Cuban sugar crop at prices substantially higher than the world market price. It may also give the Soviets another foothold in the region.

The sugar policy of the European Common Market is even worse than the American one. First, the disadvantage of European sugar production compared with that of the tropics is much greater than the American; and second, Europe has been dumping sugar in the world market. It is understandable that the poor countries greatly resent these policies of the rich industrialized countries, but if they react by stepping up their own protection, they make things worse for everybody, including themselves.

The two other pillars of development economics, the so-called demonstration effect and the hypothesis of "disguised unemployment" in poor countries, fare no better than the Prebisch-Singer theory—and both originated in the industrialized countries.

The Demonstration Effect

The theory of the demonstration effect asserts that intimate knowledge of the lifestyles in rich countries, through exposure to travel, film, radio, television, etc., encourages the people of poor countries to buy beyond their means. Thus the propensity to save is reduced and the propensity to import increased. This theory was used in the early postwar period to help explain the alleged permanent dollar shortage. The theory postulated that when the impoverished people of war-torn Europe came in contact with the United States, they tried to emulate American consumption habits; consequently, the propensity to save declined and import demand soared. However, the permanent dollar shortage did not materialize. And even apart from that, the reaction of the people in Europe was quite different from that anticipated by the theory. Consider for example, the case of Germany, the country that suffered most from aerial bombardment and ground fighting.

After wartime controls were abolished in 1948 and a market economy was established, people set to work to repair roads, reconstruct bridges, restore electric power and railroads, and rebuild bombed-out cities. True, American aid under the Marshall Plan helped, but the largest portion of the huge investment was financed domestically. Germany's ability to do so implies that saving was exceptionally large, not small, as the demonstration theory would postulate.

In poor countries, the demonstration effect greatly underestimates the intelligence and responsiveness to price changes of the common people, even of poor farmers, as Peter Bauer has shown.[9] Where the demonstration effect really operates is in the area of public policy. All too often policy markers in the developing countries seem to be more attracted and influenced by the vices of policy in the developed countries than by their virtues.

Over time, the demonstration theory has been elaborated in various ways. One case is the so-called two-gap approach to the problem of development, which was popular in the 1960s among development economists at the World Bank. According to this view, developing countries "typically," although with some notable exceptions, run into "intractable" bottlenecks or gaps that require government action. The first is the saving-investment gap, which results from the demonstration effect and the alleged fixed proportionality (rectangular isoquants) of factors of production—labor and capital. The latter assumption is also an ingredient of the theory of disguised unemployment, which will be taken up presently. The second gap is the export-import or balance-of-payments gap, which is supposed to be due to the inelasticity of the industrialized countries' demand for the exports (primary products) of the developing countries.

This is, however, a very weak argument, for the following reason: the assumption that global demand for the exports of a single country or of a group of countries may be inelastic ("elasticity pessimism" as it has been dubbed) has a long history. It has been one of the premises of the theory of the permanent dollar shortage and of other fallacies. It has been refuted many times, "Nothing approaching this has ever occurred in the real world," as Alfred Marshall once put it.

Disguised Unemployment, the Keynesian Influence

In my lectures I have mentioned that the concept of disguised unemployment originated in Keynesian circles; Joan Robinson seems to have been the first to speak of disguised unemployment, referring to workers who during the depression lost well-paying jobs in industry and subsequently did menial work to eke out a miserable living. I have also discussed the impact of Keynesianism on economic thinking and economic policy in the developing countries.

On this point there is disagreement between Ronald Findlay and myself. In his most generous and constructive comments on my *Pioneers* lecture, Findlay attributed to me the view that "the pernicious influence of Keynes" was not only responsible for "inflation and macroeconomic instability in the West," but also "infected development policy in the developing countries." This is not my position, although there is one important issue where Keynes had an important and harmful influence on development theory and policy in developing countries: his misinterpretation of the Great Depression of the 1930s as a basic flaw of capitalism which was, as we have seen, carried on by Raúl Prebisch.

In general, when speaking of the influence of Keynesian thinking, one should distinguish between Keynesian economics and the economics of Keynes. Keynesian economics refers to the views and policy recommendations of the numerous influential radical followers of Keynes who ignore the dangers of inflation. Keynes himself often changed his mind, sometimes so fast that most of his followers could not keep up. A striking example is that in 1937, one year after the publication of *The General Theory*, Keynes argued in three famous articles in *The Times* that monetary policy should shift from fighting unemployment to curbing inflation, even though unemployment was still over 10 percent and inflation was modest by later post-World War II standards. He did not, of course, give up the quest for full employment, but he made it clear that he was prepared to accept some temporary increase in unemployment in order to curb inflation.[10]

In my *Pioneers* lecture I have noted that the more sophisticated proponents of the theory of disguised unemployment in poor countries make it clear that it is not equivalent to Keynesian mass unemployment in depressions, which is curable by government deficit spending. They nevertheless assert that in the more densely populated countries in Asia, Africa, or even prewar Eastern Europe there are large pools of excess labor in rural areas (the figure of 25 percent is often mentioned) that can be withdrawn without any loss of output. This estimate is based on the assumption that the capital-labor ratio is fixed (rectangular isoquants). In my earlier writings I expressed strong doubts that this was realistic. I am pleased that my suspicion was confirmed by Nobel Laureate Theodore Schultz. Schultz states: "The doctrine that a part of the labor working in agriculture in poor countries has a marginal productivity of zero... rests on shaky theoretical presumptions," and cites as evidence the effects on agricultural production caused by the Indian influenza epidemic of 1918- 1919.[11]

Trade Policy of LDCs

I have little to add to my lectures on trade and exchange rate policy of developing countries. I still believe that the neoclassical paradigm fully applies to the developing countries. I reject the theory of two economies, one for the LDCs, the other for the developed countries. Most trade theorists lean toward free trade, but all of them admit that there are exceptions to the free-trade rule. In other words, there are theoretically valid arguments for a certain amount of protection. The two most important ones are the terms of trade or optimum tariff argument and the infant industry-external economies argument for protection. The latter naturally appeals to developing countries.

I now believe that I went too far, especially in my Cairo lectures, in trying to find justification for a certain amount of protectionism in the LDCs. It is one thing to prove theoretically that a certain amount of protection, or import substitution as it is often euphemistically called, can be justified; it is an entirely different and much more difficult thing to carry out such a policy efficiently. Anyone who is familiar with the theoretical discussions of the infant industry argument for protection will understand that the selection of suitable cases for protection and the determination of the proper dosage is a very difficult task.

As I see it, there are two major stumbling blocks to a tolerably efficient solution of the problem. First, in developing as well as in developed countries, vested interests and national prejudices for protection are very strong and make it almost impossible to eliminate a tax or a quota on imports when a mistake has been made. Second, the administrative capabilities of governments in most developing countries are notoriously weak. There are, of course, many functions that, either naturally or traditionally, are reserved for the government. These functions are vital for economic development and require heavy investments in areas such as education, law and order, transportation, and communications. Governments should concentrate on these tasks and not squander their limited managerial resources on a policy of import restriction that in practice is bound to be counterproductive.

Excessive Pessimism

In my Pioneers lecture I said that most of the development literature, both private and official, is imbued with excessive pessimism about past performance and future prospects for the poor countries. I quoted the late Simon Kuznets, who flatly contradicted the prevailing pessimism. He wrote: "Even in this recent twenty-five year period... less developed (but excepting the few countries and periods marked by internal conflicts and political breakdown), material returns have grown, per capita, at a rate higher than ever observed in the past," and he attributed the "negative reaction to economic attainments" to "a rise in expectations." To some extent the pessimism may be regarded as a negotiating stance; for much of the literature, even the unofficial literature, is meant to support demands of the poor countries for foreign aid and other concessions from the rich industrial countries. Kuznets wrote in the late 1970s, but his findings have been confirmed by later researchers using data that has become available since his death.[12]

In the past two years the pessimism about the prospects of the Third World countries has deepened. The two main reasons are the debt crisis that erupted in Mexico in 1986, and the rising pessimism and growing fear of a world depression that started even before the crash of international stock exchanges in October 1987.

On the LDC debt problem I will confine myself to a few remarks on the three largest debtors—Argentina, Brazil, and Mexico. Argentina, a country richly endowed with a good climate and natural and human resources, has really no business being less developed. Fifty years ago Colin Clark in his pioneering work *Conditions of Economic Progress* compared Argentina with Australia and predicted that its per capita income would rise along with that of Australia. Not an unreasonable prediction, but it did not happen. Why? The answer is political instability and economic mismanagement by successive regimes, beginning with the dictatorship of Colonel Peron (1941– 1952). Peron pushed industrialization and coddled labor unions at the expense of highly efficient agriculture. The consequence has been waves of high inflation incompatible with rapid growth. This problem is not an economic one, for it is well known how to stop inflation. The problem is political—how to muster the political will to do what is necessary.

Brazil and Mexico have done quite well, but they too have gotten into an inflationary rut in the past year or two. I repeat, the problem is political. Everybody knows how to stop inflation, and if anyone needs a refresher course, the experts of the IMF will be happy to provide it.

As I have mentioned, there was growing pessimism about the prospects of the United States and the world economy even before the crash on the stock exchange in October 1987. Ravi Batra's gloomy book *The Great Depression of 1990* has remained on the list of best sellers, and Stephen Marris has reconfirmed his long-standing prediction that the dollar would collapse with dire consequences for the world economy.[13]

The October 1987 crash on the stock exchange naturally deepened the pessimism. Black Monday, October 19, 1987, ominously resembled Black Tuesday, October 29, 1929, when the crash on the New York Stock Exchange ushered in the Great Depression of the 1930s.

Seven years ago I wrote a paper "The Great Depression of the 1930s: Can It Happen Again?"[14]I then argued, and I still believe, that it is unlikely for a present-day decline of economic activity that would even remotely resemble the Great Depression—when unemployment rose to 25 percent and industrial production plunged by over 50 percent. The Great Depression was not a regular decline of the business cycle, but was due to horrendous policy mistakes in the United States and other countries. I will restate a few. The most significant mistake was committed by the Federal Reserve, which let the money stock contract by 30 percent. Under fixed exchange rates—the gold standard—this deep depression in the dominant American economy was bound to spread to the rest of the Western world. The Smoot-Hawley tariff enacted during the Hoover administration intensified the world depression; and the mismanagement of the business cycle upswing that started in 1933 by Roosevelt's New Deal led to a short but extremely vicious slump in 1937–1938. Similar mistakes were made in other countries. In Germany, Chancellor H. Bruning deflated the economy deliberately in order to eliminate reparations. The resulting 40 percent unemployment, helped bring Hitler to power and gave him an opportunity for early economic successes which, in turn, greatly strengthened his regime.

It is inconceivable that such capital mistakes will be made again. I conclude there will be no decline in economic activity comparable to the Great Depression of the 1930s or earlier ones. Still, a recession is a distinct possibility and the slump in stock prices has increased that likelihood.

The United States has had seven recessions since World War II, each of them mild when compared with the Great Depression of the 1930s. In retrospect, a setback of that kind is not regarded as a calamity. But when it occurs, especially after a long period of expansion, it looks ominous and may give rise to misguided policy reactions—for example, protectionist measures or excessive monetary expansion leading to inflation and a subsequent more serious recession. However, in the present paper I cannot delve deep into the problem of the business cycle. I confine myself to a few concluding remarks.

Conclusion

The business cycle has not been abolished. Some fluctuations of output and employment are inherent in the free market—the private enterprise economy. The fluctuations can be mitigated by the judicious use of automatic stabilizers—for example, running government budget deficits in recessions when tax revenues decline and certain outlays, such as unemployment benefits, increase. Furthermore, it is most desirable to improve the economy's ability to adjust to structural changes by breaking down barriers to the movement of factors of production, (especially in the labor market?), making wages more flexible, curbing the power of labor unions, or adopting the Japanese system of paying a large part of workers' income in the form of bonuses which increase when profits rise and shrink when profits decline. But trying to suppress fluctuations altogether would be counterproductive. It would cause inflation and require increasingly stringent regulations and controls rapidly approaching comprehensive central planning. Over the past twenty years there have been many opportunities to observe the poor economic performance of communist countries in relation to that of Western countries with similar basic structures and backgrounds. These observations show that central planning is not the answer to the economic problems. Years ago Winston Churchill expressed it succinctly. "Under capitalism," he said, "wealth is distributed unequally. Under socialism misery is shared by all!" Actually, it turns out that misery, too, is shared unequally.

THE CAIRO LECTURES:

International Trade and Economic Development

First Lecture

Ladies and Gentlemen:

I regard it as a signal honor that you have invited me to give three lectures in this series which has been made famous among economists all over the world by the contributions of earlier speakers—such as F. A. v. Hayek, Per Jacobsson, Arthur Lewis, G. Myrdal, Ragnar Nurkse, to mention only a few. I am all too conscious of the fact that my illustrious forerunners in this series

The Cairo Lectures, Fiftieth Anniversary Commemoration Lectures, National Bank of Egypt, Cairo, 1959. Reprinted with permission of the author.

as well as the high position of the institution, the National Bank of Egypt, and its officers, under whose auspices these lectures are being given, have put me under a very heavy obligation. However hard I try, I am afraid, I shall not be able fully to discharge this heavy debt.

I.

As a topic for my lectures I have chosen *Economic Development and International Trade*. I shall discuss the contribution, positive or negative, favorable or unfavorable, which foreign trade can make to the economic development of underdeveloped countries. I shall make a special effort to bring the tools of economic theory, i.e., the theory of international trade, to bear upon the problem at hand and shall also draw some policy conclusions from my analysis.

What I have to say will, to some extent, be critical and polemical. But since widespread misconceptions have greatly and in my opinion perniciously influenced policy, I regard criticism of these views as a highly constructive task.

For the purposes of our discussion I shall conform to the general usage and define development as the growth of per capita real income. A factor or institution or policy—international trade or a change of trade or trade policy, free trade or protection—are said to be conducive to economic development, if it can be shown that they speed up the rate of growth of per capita real income as compared with the rate that would be obtained in the absence of the factor or policy or institution in question.

I should like to say, however, in passing that the level of per capita real income is not always a sufficient criterion to decide whether a country should be said to belong to the "developed" or "underdeveloped" part of the world. In fact, it is not easy at all to give a precise and acceptable definition. If we were satisfied with a mere enumeration of the developed and underdeveloped countries, there would be little disagreement. The economically underdeveloped part of the world consists of the Western Hemisphere south of the Rio Grande, Central and South America (with one or two exceptions), most of Asia and Africa, excepting Japan, the Union of South Africa, and one or two other countries. But when it comes to framing a formal definition and to giving precise criteria of development and underdevelopment, we run into difficulties and controversies.

Let me pursue the matter a little further, although it would be, in my opinion, a mistake to worry about the lack of a precise definition. The following statement by one of the great mathematicians and philosophers of our time may comfort you, as it did me. Hermann Weyl, in his celebrated book *Philosophy of Mathematics and Natural Science*,[1] speaking of the natural sciences, in the context in question especially of the biological sciences, says that it often happens in scientific pursuits that "the typical may be elusive in terms of well-defined concepts and yet we handle it with intuitive certitude, e.g., in recognizing persons." Surely, what is good for the natural sciences should also satisfy the social scientist.

Per capita real national income as criterion for the comparative level of development of different countries is often grossly misleading because of the difficulties and ambiguities of international income comparisons; it would be easy to cite examples of naive, misleading or even fraudulent comparisons of national income figures for different countries. But even waiving statistical difficulties of measurement and assuming that we have developed meaningful and comparable measures of real per capita income of different countries, the level of economic development of a country in a basic sense cannot always be accurately gauged by its results in terms of output. Suppose Country A is highly developed in the sense that its population is highly educated, well trained, reliable, efficient in the use of modern means and methods of production—this is what I call real, genuine development—and suppose, furthermore, that Country B is not highly developed in that sense, but is better endowed than A with natural resources, mineral deposits, good soil and climate and so on per head of its population; then it is quite possible that the less developed country will enjoy a higher per capita income than the more developed country.

It is true that a well trained, hard working and frugal people can make up to an astonishing degree for lack of natural resources as the example of Switzerland shows. Nonetheless, it would be a mistake to expect a perfect correlation between the real level of development and output per head. It would be an even greater mistake to identify the level of development with the degree of industrialization, especially in the sense of having a large percentage of the working force employed in the manufacturing ("secondary") industries. Urbanization and having a large percentage of the working population employed in "tertiary" industries, i.e., in service industries such as education, entertainment, research, scientific and artistic pursuits, is probably a much better indicator of economic development than industrialization proper.[2]

It is true there may not yet exist an underdeveloped country that is highly industrialized. But some underdeveloped countries seem to be on the way to that status, and the results are not happy. Argentina, e.g., has managed to hurt its thriving agriculture badly and has steadily been going down, financially and economically, during the regime of Colonel Peron. On the other hand, there may be no developed country in existence at the present time that is not industrialized in the sense that a large percentage of the labor force or population (the two measures are not quite the same because of the large families one finds often in the country) is in industry, mining and especially services. But some countries were highly developed before they ceased to be predominantly agricultural. New Zealand, Denmark and Australia are examples and there is nothing backward and underdeveloped about Nebraska and Iowa, American states that are predominantly agricultural. It is an extremely important fact that there exists no highly developed country that has not also a highly developed agriculture in the sense of a high degree of literacy, efficient application of modern methods of production, high input of machinery, fertilizer, etc. and high value of output per head.[3] Moreover, and this too is a very important fact, many highly industrialized countries (in the sense that a large percentage of the labor force is engaged in non-agricultural pursuits), have remained large net exporters of food and agricultural raw materials. The U.S., Canada, Australia, and Denmark are conspicuous examples.

These facts have important policy implications which are often ignored. The fact that in developed countries not only industry, but also agriculture, is more highly developed than in underdeveloped countries lends further weight to the warning that development policies should not concentrate exclusively on industry. And the fact that highly industrialized countries can remain efficient producers and cheap exporters of food and agricultural raw material should help to dispel the fear that it would be dangerous for industrial countries to fill a large share of their food and agricultural raw material requirements from foreign sources (possibly from underdeveloped countries) and to give up a correspondingly large part of their own high cost agriculture, on the ground that if they did that, later when industrialization has proceeded farther in many parts of the world, they may not be able to buy food and agricultural raw materials except at exorbitant prices.[4] Such fears were widespread among German economists around the turn of the century when Germany was making rapid strides towards industrialization. But one finds them also occasionally today. They are, e.g., implicit in certain versions of the Marxian theory (espoused also by non-Marxist writers such as G. Myrdal) that the underdeveloped countries of today are handicapped as compared with the now developed countries in the corresponding stage of their development because the underdeveloped countries today, when they push their development (identified, by those writers, with industrialization) are not surrounded by an underdeveloped world, as the now developed countries were in the early stages of their development—an underdeveloped world which provided industrializing countries with cheap supplies of raw material and food and a market for their industrial products. If my strictures draw the reply that it was the colonial status of the *then* underdeveloped countries which gave the now developed countries their comparative advantage over the underdeveloped countries *now*, my answer would be this: I am not going to discuss to what extent colonial rule has exploited the colonies and retarded their development. To some extent and in some cases it has undoubtedly done that. Not being an expert in that area, I shall not try to make any generalization. And fortunately I need not form a judgment on that matter because for the problem at hand another question is crucial, namely, the question to what extent the development of the colonial powers themselves was speeded by their possession of colonies. With respect to this question, I feel much more confident. My answer is that the possession of colonies was not a decisive or even very important factor in the development of the colonial powers. If it had been, it would be difficult to explain why colonial powers have done quite well after having lost their colonies (e.g. the Netherlands) and why other countries such as Germany,[5] Sweden, Switzerland, not to mention the USA, which never possessed colonies (or whose colonies were economically unimportant) developed just as well, or better, than others that had colonies.

But let me return to my main topic—the contribution of international trade to economic development. In this context growth of real income or output per head can be used with greater confidence as criterion, than in connection with the question as to which countries should be regarded as developed or underdeveloped, for in this case no intra-country comparisons are involved.[6]

II.

I shall now positively and systematically state what I think the contribution of international trade to economic development was in the past and what it can be in the future. My overall conclusion is that international trade has made a tremendous contribution to the development of less developed countries in the 19th and 20th centuries and can be expected to make an equally big contribution in the future, if it is allowed to proceed freely. It does not necessarily follow that a 100 percent free trade policy is always most conducive to most rapid development. Marginal interferences with the free flow of trade, if properly selected, may speed up development. But I do not want to leave any doubt that my conclusion is that substantially free trade with marginal, insubstantial corrections and deviations, is the best policy from the point of view of economic development. Drastic deviations from free trade can be justified, on development grounds—and this is very nearly the same thing as to say on economic grounds—only if and when they are needed to compensate for the adverse influence of other policies inimical to economic development, for example, the consequences of persistent inflation or of certain tax and domestic price support policies. Let me guard against a possible misunderstanding. If I say that drastic interferences with the market mechanism are not needed for rapid development, I refer to trade policy and I do not deny that drastic measures in other areas, let me say, land reform, education, forced investment (if the projects are well chosen) etc. may not speed up growth. But I shall in these lectures not further elaborate on those matters.[7]

I shall make use of the so-called classical theory of international trade in its neoclassical form associated with the name of Jacob Viner, James Meader, and Bertil Ohlin, to mention only a few. I shall not try to modernize the theory more than, say, Ohlin and Meade have done, although I shall make an attempt to spell out in some detail the implications of classical trade theory for economic development, an aspect which has perhaps been somewhat neglected. On the other hand, I shall, of course, avoid using the caricature of the theory which is often presented as a portrait by its critics.

Later I shall then take up in detail objections to the orthodox conclusions and shall consider alternative or rival theories put forward by the critics of the orthodox theory.

Let us then start with first things first. International division of labor and international trade, which enable every country to specialize and to export those things that it can produce cheaper in exchange for what others can provide at a lower cost, have been and still are one of the basic factors promoting economic well-being and increasing national income of every participating country. Moreover, what is good for the national income and the standard of living is, at least potentially, also good for economic development; for the greater the volume of output the greater can be the rate of growth—provided the people individually or collectively have the urge to save and to invest and economically to develop. The higher the level of output, the easier it is to escape the "vicious circle of poverty" and to "take off into selfsustained growth" to use the jargon of modern development theory. Hence, if trade raises the level of income, it also promotes economic development.

All this holds for highly developed countries as well as for less developed ones. Let us not forget that countries in the former category, too, develop and grow, some of them—not all—even faster than some—not all—in the second category.

In most underdeveloped countries international trade plays quantitatively an especially important role—that is, a larger percentage of their income is spent on imports, and a larger percentage of their output is being exported, than in the case of developed countries of comparable economic size. (Other things being equal, it is natural that the "larger," economically speaking, a country, the smaller its trade percentages.) Many underdeveloped countries are highly specialized also in the sense that a very large percentage of their exports consists of one or two staple commodities. I am sure that here in Egypt, which depends on cotton for more than 60 percent of its exports, I need not cite further examples for that.

This high concentration of exports is not without danger. One would normally not want to put so many of one's eggs into one basket. But the price of diversification is in most cases extremely high. I shall touch on that topic once more. At this point, let me simply say that a high level of concentrated trade will, in most cases, be much better than a low level of diversified trade. How much poorer would Brazil be without coffee, Venezuela, Iran and Iraq without oil, Bolivia without tin, Malaya without rubber and tin, Ghana without cocoa, and I dare say, Egypt without cotton. The really great danger of concentration arises in the case of deep and protracted slumps in the industrial countries—slumps of the order of magnitude of the Great Depression in the 1930s. In my opinion, and here I am sure the overwhelming majority of economists in the Western World agrees, the chance that this will happen again is practically nil.

The tremendous importance of trade for the underdeveloped countries (as well as for most developed ones, with the exception of the US and the USSR, which could, if need be, give it up without suffering a catastrophic reduction in their living standard) follows from the classical theory of comparative cost in conjunction with the fact that the comparative differences in cost of production of industrial products and food and raw materials between developed countries and underdeveloped countries are obviously very great, in many cases, in fact, infinite in the sense that countries of either group just could not produce what they buy from the other.[8]

The classical theory has been often criticized on the ground that it is static, that it presents only a timeless "cross-section" view of comparative costs and fails to take into account dynamic elements that is, the facts of organic growth and development. Of modern writers, it was especially Professor J. H. Williams of Harvard and recently Gunnar Myrdal[9] who have voiced this criticism of the classical doctrine and have demanded its replacement by a dynamic theory. This type of criticism is, in fact, about as old as the classical theory itself. Williams mentions many earlier critics and especially the German writer Frederich List who more than anyone else in the 19th century has attacked the classical theory on exactly the same grounds, that is, for being "unhistorical and static,"[10] with the same vehemence and the same strange tone of bitterness and irritation as the modern writers.

Now it is true that the theory of comparative cost is static; it is also true that the economies of most countries are changing and developing and that the theory should take account of that fact. But it is not true that a static theory, because it is static, is debarred from saying anything useful about a changing and developing economic world. There is such a thing as "comparative statics," that is, a method for dealing with a changing situation by means of a static theory. How much can be done by means of comparative statics (as distinguished from a truly dynamic theory) depends on the type of problem at hand. I contend that the problems of international division of labor and long-run development are such that the method of comparative statics can go a long way towards a satisfactory solution.[11] That does not mean, however, that a dynamic theory would not be very useful. Unfortunately, not much of a truly dynamic theory is available at present. What the critics of the static nature of traditional theory have given us over and above their criticism and methodological pronouncements is very little indeed and thoroughly unsatisfactory. But a well known Burmese economist, H. Myint, has recently reminded us that the classical economists, especially Adam Smith and J. S. Mill, were by no means oblivious of the indirect, dynamic benefits which less developed countries in particular can derive from international trade. Going beyond the purely static theory of comparative cost, they have analyzed the "indirect effects" of trade (as J. S. Mill calls them) and thereby presented us with at least the rudiments of a dynamic theory, which Myint aptly calls the "productivity" theory of international trade.[12] Let us then inquire how we can deal, by means of the theoretical tools on hand, with the problems of change and development. The tools on hand are the static theory of comparative cost and the semi-dynamic "productivity" theory.

For our purposes I will distinguish two types of changes which constitute economic development—those that take place independently of international trade, and those that are induced by trade or trade policy.

As far as the first group—let me call them autonomous changes— is concerned, I can see no difficulty resulting from them for the applicability of the classical theory of comparative cost. Such changes are the gradual improvement in skill, education and training of workers, farmers, engineers, entrepreneurs; improvements resulting from inventions and discoveries and from the accumulation of capital—changes which in the Western World stem for the most part from the initiative of individuals and private associations, but possibly also from conscious Government policies.[13]

These changes come gradually or in waves and result in gradually increasing output of commodities that had been produced before or in the setting up of production of goods that had not been produced earlier. Analytically, such development has to be pictured as an outward movement of the production possibility curve (often called substitution or transformation curve). Depending on the concrete turn that autonomous development (including improvements in transportation technology) takes, the comparative cost situation and hence volume and composition of trade will be more or less profoundly affected. But since these changes only come slowly and gradually and usually cannot be foreseen (either by private business or Government planners) in sufficient detail to make anticipatory action possible, there is no presumption that the allocative mechanism as described in the theory of comparative cost will not automatically and efficiently bring about the changes and adjustment in the volume and structure of trade called for by autonomous development.

I turn now to the second type of changes in the productive capabilities of a country which are more important for the purposes of my lectures, namely, those induced by trade and changes in trade including changes in trade brought about by trade policy. Favorable as well as unfavorable trade-induced changes are possible and have to be considered. Alleged unfavorable trade-induced changes have received so much attention from protectionist writers from List to Myrdal (which has induced free trade ecomomists, too, to discuss them at great length), that there is danger that the tremendously important favorable influences be unduly neglected. Let me, therefore, discuss the latter first.

If we were to estimate the contribution of international trade to economic development, especially of the underdeveloped countries, solely by the static gains from trade in any given year on the usual assumption of given[14] production capabilities (analytically under the assumption of given production functions or given or autonomously shifting production possibility curves) we could indeed grossly underrate the importance of trade. For over and above the direct static gains dwelt upon by the traditional theory of comparative cost, trade bestows very important indirect benefits, which also can be described as dynamic benefits, upon the participating countries. Let me emphasize once more that the older classical writers did stress these "indirect benefits" (Mill's own words).[15] Analytically we have to describe these "indirect," "dynamic" benefits from trade as an outward shift (in the northeast direction) of the production possibility curve brought about by a trade-induced movement along the curve.

First, trade provides material means (capital goods, machinery and raw and semifinished materials) indispensable for economic development. Secondly, even more important, trade is the means and vehicle for the dissemination of technological knowledge, the transmission of ideas, for the importation of know-how, skills, managerial talents and entrepreneurship. Thirdly, trade is also the vehicle for the international movement of capital especially from the developed to the underdeveloped countries. Fourthly, free international trade is the best antimonopoly policy and the best guarantee for the maintenance of a healthy degree of free competition.

Let me now make a few explanatory remarks on each of these four points before I try to show how they fit into, and complement, the static theory of comparative advantage.

The first point is so obvious that it does not require much elaboration. Let us recall and remember, however, the tremendous benefits which the underdeveloped countries draw from technological progress in the developed countries through the importation of machinery, transport equipment, vehicles, power generation equipment, road building machinery, medicines, chemicals, and so on. The advantage is, of course, not all on one side. I stress the advantage derived by underdeveloped countries (rather than the equally important benefits for the developed countries), because I am concerned in these lectures primarily with the development of the less developed countries.

The composition of the export trade of the developed industrial countries has been changing, as we all know, in the direction of the types of capital goods which I have mentioned away from textiles and other light consumer goods. This shift has been going on for a long time; it is not a recent phenomenon. But it has proceeded rapidly in recent years, and there is no reason to doubt that it will continue.

Secondly, probably even more important than the importation of material goods is the importation of technical know-how, skills, managerial talents, entrepreneurship. This is, of course, especially important for the underdeveloped countries. But the developed countries too benefit greatly from cross-fertilization aided by trade among themselves and the less advanced industrial countries can profit from the superior technical and managerial know-how, etc., of the more advanced ones.

The latecomers and successors in the process of development and industrialization have always had the great advantage that they could learn from the experiences, from the successes as well as from the failures and mistakes of the pioneers and forerunners. In the late nineteenth century the continental European countries and the U.S. profited greatly from the technological innovation and achievements of the industrial revolution in Great Britain. Later the Japanese proved to be very adept learners and Soviet Russia has shown herself capable of speeding up her own development by "borrowing" (interest free) immense amounts of technological know-how from the West, developing it further and adopting it for her own purposes. This "trade" has been entirely one-sided. I know of not a single industrial idea or invention which the West has obtained from the East.[16] Today the underdeveloped countries have a tremendous, constantly growing, store of technological know-how to draw from. True, simple adoption of methods developed for the conditions of the developed countries is often not possible. But adaptation is surely much easier than first creation.

Trade is the most important vehicle for the transmission of technological know-how. True, it is not the only one. In fact this function of trade is probably somewhat less important now than it was a hundred years ago, because ideas, skills, know-how, travel easier and quicker and cheaper today than in the nineteenth century. The market where engineering and management experts can be hired is much better organized than formerly. There is much more competition in this field as well as in the area of material capital equipment. In the early nineteenth century Great Britain was the only center from which industrial equipment and know-how could be obtained, and there were all sorts of restrictions on the exportation of both. Today there are a dozen industrial centers in Europe, the U.S., Canada, and Japan, and even Russia and Czechoslovakia, all ready to sell machinery as well as engineering advice and know-how.

However, trade is still the most important transmission belt. What J. S. Mill said 100 years ago is still substantially true: "It is hardly possible to overrate the value in the present low state of human improvement, of placing human beings in contact with persons dissimilar to themselves, and with modes of thought and action unlike those with which they are familiar. . . Such communication has always been, peculiarly in the present age one of the primary sources of progress."[17]

The third indirect benefit of trade which I mentioned was that it also serves as a transmission belt for capital. It is true that the amount of capital that an underdeveloped country can obtain from abroad depends in the first place on the ability and willingness of developed countries to lend, which is of course decisively influenced by the internal policies in the borrowing countries. But it stands to reason—and this is the only point I wanted to make at this juncture—that, other things being equal, the larger the volume of trade, the greater will be the volume of foreign capital that can be expected to become available under realistic assumptions. The reason is that with a large volume of trade the transfer of interest and repayments on principle is more easily effected than with a small volume of trade; and it would be clearly unrealistic to expect large capital movements if the chance for transfer of interests and repayments is not good. There is, furthermore, the related fact that it is much easier to get foreign capital for export industries with their built-in solution of the retransfer problem than for other types of investments which do not directly and automatically improve the balance of payments. This preference of foreign capital for export industries is regrettable because other types of investment (such as investment in public utilities, railroads, manufacturing industries) may often (not always) be more productive and may make a greater indirect contribution, dollar per dollar, to economic development by providing training to native personnel and in various other ways than export industries which sometimes (by no means always) constitute foreign enclaves in native soil. If the direct and indirect contribution of non-export industries to national income and economic development are in fact greater than those of the export industry, they should be preferred, because their indirect contribution to the balance of payments position will then also be such as to guarantee the possibility of smooth retransfer of principle and interest—*provided* inflationary monetary policies do not upset equilibrium entailing exchange control that then gets in the way of the transfer. But with inflationary monetary policies and exchange control practices as they are in most underdeveloped countries, the preference of foreign capital for export industries is readily understandable and must be reckoned with and foreign capital in export is better than no foreign capital at all.

The fourth way in which trade benefits a country indirectly is by fostering healthy competition and keeping in check inefficient monopolies. The reason why the American economy is more competitive—and often more efficient—than most others is probably to be sought more in the great internal free trade area which the U.S. enjoys rather than in the antimonopoloy policy which was always much more popular in the U.S. than in Europe or anywhere else. The importance of this factor is confirmed by the fact that many experts believe that the main economic advantages of the European Common Market, towards the realization of which the first steps have just been taken, will flow from freer competition rather than merely from the larger size and larger scale production which it entails.

Increased competition is important also for underdeveloped countries, especially inasmuch as the size of their market is usually small (even if the geographic area is large). A reservation has nevertheless to be made. The first introduction of new industries on infant industry grounds may justify the creation of monopolistic positions, depending on the size of the country and the type of industry. But the problem will always remain how to prevent the permanent establishment of inefficient exploitative monopolies even after an industry has taken root and has become able to hold its ground without the crutches of import restrictions.

The general conclusion, then, is that international trade, in addition to the static gains resulting from the division of labor with given (or autonomously changing) production functions, powerfully contributes, in the four ways indicated, to the development of the productive capabilities of the less developed countries. Analytically, we have to express that, in the framework of modern trade theory, by saying that trade gradually transforms existing production functions; in other words, that a movement along the production possibility curves in accordance with the pre-existing comparative cost situation, will tend to push up and out the production possibility curve.

I have stated my conclusions rather boldly and uncompromisingly. Some qualifications and reservations are obviously called for, because trade may have also unfavorable indirect (or direct) effects. But I shall discuss these exceptions and qualifications after I have discussed and considered opposing views.

Second Lecture

In my first lecture I presented the case for a maximum of international trade in the interest of economic development. I started with the static theory of comparative cost but pointed out that the classical economists especially Adam Smith and John Stuart Mill were not oblivious to indirect dynamic influences of international trade. International trade not only increases national income within given production functions, thereby enabling a country to save and invest more, but trade also increases productive capabilities, analytically speaking, pushes out production functions and production possibility curves. I distinguished four different ways in which trade operates to bring that about. (1) It enables a country to import capital goods of all description which are needed for economic development. (2) Trade serves as a transmission belt for the dissemination of ideas, technological know-how, skills, managerial and entrepreneurial services. (3) Trade is the vehicle of international capital movements. (4) Free trade is the most effective antimonopoloy policy; in other words, trade makes for healthy competition.

My conclusion was that free trade is extremely desirable from the point of view of economic development especially of the underdeveloped countries.

III.

I am aware that my conclusions are not shared by everybody. In fact, influential experts, both academic and official, as well as certain branches of the United Nations, have been contending almost the exact opposite of what I have been trying to say. I shall now consider those opposing views and while, by and large, after careful weighing of evidence and arguments, I shall stick to my conclusions, certain not negligible qualifications and reservations will have to be made.

While I have sung the praise of international trade as a factor spurring the rate of economic development, especially in the less developed countries, I must voice a warning against certain exaggerations. There are certain things trade cannot do. No amount of trade can be expected to bring about a complete or even a nearly complete equalization of real wages or more generally of real per capita income as between different countries and areas. It is not even certain that trade will in all cases result in a lessening of the existing degree of international inequality (assuming that an unambiguous measure of degrees of inequality as between different countries can be agreed upon).

Contrary to what is sometimes said, even by experts,[18] classical or neo-classical theory does *not* teach that free trade will result in international equalization of real income. What the theory does teach is that everybody will be better off with trade than without trade and that every country will be best served by free trade. Needless to add that the latter conclusion, the free trade conclusion, is subject to important exceptions and qualifications. There hardly exists a single free trade economist who does not recognize certain exceptions to the rule that free trade is the best commercial policy and it is widely accepted that in less developed countries the exceptions are more numerous and important than in the advanced industrial countries.

It is true that in recent years a highly abstract discussion has been carried on in the learned journals in the course of which some participants thought they were able to prove that under certain assumptions free commodity trade would be a perfect substitute for free international migration of labor and free movement of factors of production in general and would thus lead to complete equalization of factor prices as between the trading countries. But the assumptions necessary for that happy result proved to be much more restrictive and unrealistic than was at first thought. So that theoretical flurry really wound up with the opposite conclusion of the one that was at first announced: it has shown that an equalization of factor prices is in reality almost inconceivable. I shall not go into that highly esoteric disputation. It can be credited with having clarified certain theoretical puzzles, but "the factor price equalization theorem" should not be pronounced as one of the conclusions of classical trade theory. To repeat—what classical theory really teaches is that trade will benefit every country, rich and poor, but not that mere trade will necessarily remove or even reduce international inequality.

It is true that in my first lecture I have advanced reasons to the effect that underdeveloped countries are likely to derive special advantages from trade. If we lived in a static world it would follow that trade has an equalizing tendency (although not necessarily that it would lead to a *complete* equalization of incomes). In the dynamic, developing world of ours, which is subject to many other influences than those connected with international trade, there is no guarantee, even with a lot of unrestricted trade, that historically international inequalities will become smaller. In such a world it does not even follow from what has been said about the special importance of trade for the less developed countries, that international inequality will be less with trade (or with much trade) than without trade (or with little trade).

Let me mention two reasons why international inequality *may* increase (I do not say, of course, *must* increase) despite the special advantages of trade to the poorer countries. First, population pressure is stronger in many less developed countries than in most advanced countries and may even become stronger if trade leads initially to higher living standard, better health, to improved sanitation and lower mortality. It is then possible that the relatively greater advantages from trade accruing to the less developed countries may be insufficient to completely outweigh this handicap.

Secondly, the developed countries do not stand still, they too develop, and some of them even grow faster than some underdeveloped countries. Thus the greater advantage of trade for the latter countries may not completely offset for some of them the head start (not only with respect to the *level* but also with respect to the *rate of growth* of income) of some of the former.[19]

IV.

The exact opposite of the classical theory that all participating countries profit from international trade is the neo-Marxian theory to the effect that trade—capitalistic, unregulated trade of course—far from benefiting the poor countries, actually operates in such a way as to make the poor countries in the world poorer and the rich richer; according to this theory, a version of which has been adopted (or independently invented) by non-Marxist writers, the poor as a rule get poorer because the rich get richer.

I said neo-Marxist—advisedly—because Marx himself, although as you know not an ardent supporter of the capitalist system, gave the devil its due, which cannot be said of all his followers. He had a very high opinion indeed of the power of capitalism to raise productivity. In truly dithyrambic language he described in the famous *Communist Manifesto* how capitalism industrializes backward countries and increases their productive capacities.[20] Needless to add that Marx did not teach that capitalism increased the productivity of backward countries for the purpose of raising the welfare of the masses of their population. And, like the English writers of the classical school whose disciple he was, Marx was not in favor of colonialism. But an appreciation of the power of international trade and international capital movements, especially of the indirect, dynamic aspects which I discussed earlier, is implicit in Marx's position. The exploitative aspects of the theory, the theory that is to say that the gains from trade are so unequally distributed as to make trade operate to the detriment of the poorer countries, the less developed countries, the primary producing or "peripheral" countries (all these terms are now used more or less synonymously)—this part of the theory has been carried over by neo-Marxists and some non-Marxists into the post-colonial period.

You will remember that Marx taught that under capitalism in each country the working class, the proletariat, was getting poorer all the time. This "theory of increasing misery" ("Verelendungstheorie") has more or less grudgingly and reluctantly (more often silently rather than explicitly) been given up, even by orthodox Marxists; for it simply makes no sense to say that American or European workers are getting poorer all the time. But the theory of increasing misery survives in the international sphere; here it has even been adopted, or independently invented, by non-Marxist writers.[21] I shall examine, however, only the non-Marxist version of the theory that "trade operates (as a rule) with a fundamental bias in favor of the richer and progressive regions (and countries) and in disfavor of other regions" (i.e., underdeveloped regions and countries)[22] that "by itself freer trade would even tend to perpetuate stagnation in the underdeveloped regions" (and countries).[23]

The theory rests on several pillars which have been widely accepted as very strong several years ago, but have been badly shaken in recent years by critical examination and by new empirical evidence that has been turned up by later experience and research. Let me briefly discuss the following three pillars of the modern theory of the pernicious effect of international trade on less developed countries.

The first is the alleged tendency of unregulated trade to turn the terms of trade in the long run against the primary producers and to impart to them an excessive cyclical instability. Secondly, there is the assertion that trade creates or at least perpetuates, or at any rate is unable to eradicate, and take advantage of, disguised unemployment. Thirdly, there are alleged "backsetting" (i.e., unfavorable) effects that are said to emanate from the developing industrial countries and impinge upon the underdeveloped countries. These effects are largely taken from alleged interregional developments; they are blown up beyond recognition and uncritically transferred to the international scene.

The theory of the secular tendency of the terms of trade to deteriorate for primary producers, i.e., for prices of primary, especially agricultural, products to fall relatively to the prices of finished goods is a big topic and raises many intricate questions. I can nevertheless be brief, because recent researches, both theoretical and statistical,[24] made it abundantly clear that the theory under review is based on grossly insufficient empirical evidence, that it has misinterpreted the facts on which it is based, that the attempted explanation of the alleged facts is fallacious and that there is no presumption at all that the alleged unfavorable tendency of the terms of trade will continue in the future.

The theory under review is generally known as the Singer-Prebisch thesis.[25] Its empirical basis is the fact that the ratio of British import prices to British export prices has fallen from 163 for 1876–80 to 100 in 1938. For the following reason, however, the improvement of the British terms of trade does not support the conclusion that the terms of trade of all exporters of primary products have suffered a corresponding deterioration.

First, as Kindleberger has shown, the British terms of trade cannot be taken as indicative of the terms of trade of all other industrial countries. Kindleberger's extensive calculations reveal large divergences between the movement of the British terms of trade and those of other industrial countries. Secondly, the British terms of trade cannot without question be taken as the reciprocal of the terms of trade of the raw material exporting countries with which Britain was trading because British import prices are taken c.i.f. and British export prices f.o.b. In other words, imports are valued including transport costs to British ports of entry and export prices excluding transport costs from British ports of exit to the foreign destination. In order to evaluate the true terms of trade of the exporters of primary products both export and import prices must be measured at the ports of entry of those countries. As Viner, Baldwin and others have pointed out, in periods in which freight rates change, such a shift of the geographical base makes a great difference for the terms of trade. Professor Ellsworth, who has investigated that problem, statistically concludes e.g., that "a large proportion, and perhaps all, of the decline in the British prices of primary products in the period between 1876 and 1905 can be attributed to the great decline in inward freight rates. . .Since the prices of British manufactured exports fell in this period by 15 percent, the terms of trade of primary countries, were f.o.b. prices used for their exports as well as for their imports, may well have moved in their favor" (loc. cit. p. 55–57). Mr. Carl Major Wright of the U.N. in a remarkable paper[26] cites numerous examples when in a period of falling import prices in Great Britain, the prices of the same goods rose in the distant ports of lading; the difference having been absorbed by falling freight rates. This was often true even of cyclical price drops. I might add that during the recent recession price declines in raw materials have been greatly softened as far as the exporters are concerned by the sharp drop in freight rates.

Thirdly, over long periods all terms of trade figures have a strong bias, because they cannot make proper allowance for changes in quality of old products and for the appearance on the market of hosts of new commodities. Since it is primarily industrial products which improve in quality while primary products remain qualitatively more or less the same and since literally hundreds of new products are added over the years to the list of finished industrial goods, this bias operates in such a way as to make the movement in the terms of trade of the primary exporters (finished goods importers) appear much less favorable than it actually was. To present but one example, let me mention that Professor Kindleberger, who computes an index of machinery prices, is forced to define the price of machines in dollars per physical weight! Hence when a machine becomes lighter and more efficient—a typical form of development—and the dollar price per machine remains unchanged, the index will indicate a price rise instead of a price fall as it should.

It follows from these considerations that it is very doubtful whether actually, over the stated period, the alleged deterioration in the terms of trade has taken place.[27] Moreover, suppose for argument's sake, the commodity terms of trade of primary producers, or of a certain group of such countries, has really deteriorated. The implications for the welfare of the country or countries concerned depend on the causes that are at the root of the change. If export prices have fallen because the cost of production has been reduced, the "deterioration" in the terms of trade has no sinister implications. For example, in the late 19th Century when the United States, Canada and Argentina gradually came into the European market with their agricultural products, the basic reason for the relative price fall of primary products was that the costs of production of the newly opened areas (including the cost of transport on land and across the ocean) had been sharply reduced (or were much lower in the first place than the cost of European competitors). Hence one cannot say that the price fall hurt the overseas suppliers although it did injure European agriculture. Economists express that by saying that what matters from the welfare standpoint is not the commodity terms of trade, but the single-factoral terms of trade. The criticized theory simply takes no notice of all this.

In the attempted explanation of the alleged facts, the theory is just as careless as in the ascertainment of what really happened. Two reasons are usually given for the alleged change in the terms of trade against primary products, (a) monopolistic manipulations in the industrial countries and (b) the operation of "Engel's law."

(a) Employers and labor unions in the industrial countries are said to conspire to keep prices up in the face of declining real cost. Thus they fail to pass on to the consumers in the form of lower prices, the fruits of technological progress, but keep them for themselves by raising wages and profits.

It is, of course, true that monetary policy in the industrial countries has not been most of the time (especially in the recent period) such as to let money wages (and money incomes in general) go up with stable or even rising prices instead of keeping money wages (incomes) constant and letting prices fall. Union policies have surely contributed to that result. But there is not the slightest indication that this policy has led to a shift in *relative* prices of primary products and finished goods. The criticized theory thus rests on a confusion of the absolute price level and relative prices. In passing, it might be pointed out that if the advanced countries followed the policy of keeping money wages constant and letting prices fall (a policy which is often recommended by conservative economists in the industrial countries) it would be definitely injurious to the less developed countries on two grounds: First, the real burden of debt would rise and second, the difference in the degree of inflationary pressure as between the two groups of countries would become even greater than it actually is—thus adding to the balance of payments woes of the less developed countries.

As far as monopolistic pricing of finished goods, either consumer or capital goods, is concerned, there is very little of it, surely less in international trade than within some of the industrial countries, and much less than there was 50 or 100 years ago. The reason for that I have mentioned before: there are now many industrial centers competing with one another in the world market. The rise of the U.S. as an industrial power has greatly contributed to making world markets more competitive because the U.S. economy has always been more competitive and U.S. industry less secretive than their European counterparts.

(b) Engel's law states that the percentage of consumer income spent on food is a decreasing function of income. When income rises people spend smaller fractions of their income on food. Inasmuch as services ("tertiary industries") become more and more important as people get richer, one can probably also say that the percentage of national income spent on raw materials (including those from mining) tends to fall.

But from this bare fact it does by no means follow that prices of primary products must fall as compared with prices of finished goods. The reason is that there are numerous counteracting and conflicting forces and tendencies at work, for example, technological changes, industrialization in the developed as well as in the underdeveloped countries, population growth and the law of diminishing returns in primary production.

It is very interesting to observe that there exists a school of thought, which teaches that the terms of trade must inexorably turn *against* the *industrial* countries because of the operation of the law of diminishing returns in agriculture and extractive industries. This theory, which has had a remarkable hold on British economic thinking, goes back to Ricardo. A. Marshall greatly worried about the terms of trade and Keynes at one time (1912) got alarmed by a deterioration of the British terms of trade.[28] In our time Professor Austin Robinson[29] again has taken up this theme.

This pessimistic theory—pessimistic from the point of view of the industrial countries—is the exact opposite of the Singer-Prebisch-Myrdal thesis. One of the strange things in this strange economic world of ours is that no one in either group seems to be aware of the fact that those in the other group say exactly the opposite and hence no one takes issue with the arguments of their opponents.

If you ask me which of the two schools is right, my answer is that both are wrong. It might be objected that this is impossible—the terms of trade cannot go in opposite directions at the same time. This, of course, is true. But let us not forget that the term of trade may not change at all or may for some time go one way and then move in the opposite direction. That is what they seem actually to have done.[30]

At any rate, it is rash to make forecasts on the basis of such flimsy foundations and it is irresponsible to recommend policies on the strength of such uncertain extrapolations. These irresponsibilities are committed by each of the two opposing schools. One recommends protection for agriculture in the advanced countries because the terms of trade will turn against the industrial countries. The other group recommends protection of industry in the less developed countries because the terms of trade will move the other way. So protectionists everywhere unite, unknowingly, on the basis of contradictory forecasts, to bring about the same result—a reduction in the volume of trade to the disadvantage of both groups of countries.

The complaint about the short run instability, especially cyclical variability of the terms of trade of raw material producers, has more substance than their alleged secular tendency to deteriorate. But the cyclical fluctuations are by no means so regular, big and pervasive as they have been pictured. Different types of raw materials and foodstuffs have been pictured. Different types of raw materials and foodstuffs have different cyclical patterns and different amplitudes. The cyclical swings are greatest in the case of metals and are greater in raw materials than in food. Even in the short run substantial relief is often afforded by a drop in freight rates during depressions.

The really serious adverse changes in the terms of trade of primary producers happen in severe depressions. But such catastrophies hit the advanced countries probably just as hard as the less developed countries, although in the form of unemployment rather than in the form of lower prices. It would be idle, however, to speculate who has fared worse on these occasions. For, let me emphasize once more, deep depressions are a thing of the past. I don't want to exaggerate. Mild recessions like the three recessions through which the American economy has passed during the postwar period will certainly recur. However deep, prolonged depressions are definitely out. There can be no doubt that the problem of creeping inflation is much more acute than that of serious depressions. I personally do not take the dangers of creeping inflation as lightly as many of my fellow economists do in the West, precisely because creeping inflation can easily lead to mild recessions and to a lower level of employment on the average over the cycle than otherwise would be the case. But severe depressions are not being tolerated any more—not even in the most capitalist countries. The problems posed by mild recessions for the exports of the less developed countries can be solved with the help of existing machinery—*ad hoc* credit arrangements through I.M.F. and other stabilization schemes. The remaining instability surely is not nearly large enough to put a serious handicap on the development in the raw material exporting countries or to call in question the immense advantages for them of unhampered international trade.

Third Lecture

In my second lecture I pointed out that, opposing the classical theory according to which free trade is beneficial to all, rich and poor, because there is a basic harmony of interests, there exists a neo-Marxian theory espoused (or independently invented) also by non-Marxist writers which postulates a basic disharmony between rich and poor, developed and underdeveloped countries. Free trade, according to this view, is inimical to the poor and an instrument of exploitation (even apart from colonialism) by the rich. The non-Marxist version of that theory rests on several pillars. The first one, the theory that the terms of trade have a tendency in the long-run to move against the primary producers, I have criticized the last time. It is, I think, the weakest of the three.

The other two pillars I shall criticize in the current lecture and then state reservations to my own free trade position which I have promised.

V.

The second pillar of the theory under consideration—the assertion that there are available in underdeveloped countries, mainly in agriculture, large masses of unused but more or less easily usable labor, "disguised unemployment"—has not fared much better than the theory of the long-run deterioration of the terms of trade. Under the criticism of economic experts in the underdeveloped as well as in developed countries, this pillar has all but collapsed. Among the early critics of the theory of disguised unemployment were men like Dr. N. Kostner, Eugenio Gudin, Professor Jacob Viner, Professor Theodore Schultz.[31] It is now admitted even by former enthusiasts that "the early easy optimism about transferring the disguised unemployed from agriculture to industry has disappeared. It is recognized that in many underdeveloped countries *static* disguised unemployment in agriculture is at a very low level. . . Substantial numbers could not be released from agriculture without a drop in agricultural production, unless the average size of holdings is increased and some degree of mechanization introduced." This statement by Professor Benjamin Higgins[32] is typical of the disillusionment that has taken place.

Professor Schultz, one of the world's foremost agricultural experts who has had wide experience in underdeveloped countries in different parts of the world, has declared flatly that he knows of no evidence for any poor country anywhere that would suggest that a transfer of even a small fraction, say, 5 percent, of the labor force from agriculture to industry could be made, other things equal, without reducing output.[33] Later he added that development "programs based on disguised unemployment have not performed as expected: instead of labor resources responding to an increase in the money supply or to new industries in the way that one would have expected if there were considerable underemployment, workers act as if the marginal productivities of laborers in agriculture and in other fields are about the same."[34]

The term "unemployment" in connection with underdeveloped, poor countries was most unfortunate indeed because it suggested that the situation is approximately the same as depression unemployment in developed countries which can be easily cured (at least up to a certain irreducible minimum) by strengthening effective demand.[35] What the proponents of the concept should have said is that in underdeveloped countries productivity of labor is very low, which is about the same as saying that those countries are desperately poor and backward; this, of course, nobody would have denied. They might have added that productivity is lower in some branches of the economy than in others. But it is surely not true to regard agriculture as the only sector of the economy where marginal productivity of labor is especially low. Dr. Kostner has pointed out to me the fact that productivity is also low (occasionally even zero or negative) in certain non-agricultural urban pursuits, as a short stroll though the streets of any city in a poor country—and in some not so poor countries—will convince even a casual observer.

Far be it from me to deny or minimize these deplorable conditions or to suggest that nothing can or should be done to improve them. But the description of the situation as disguised unemployment suggests that there is unlimited, if not efficient, then at least usable, manpower available to start new industries without reducing output anywhere else. This simply is not so. Such oversimplifications encourage easy solutions which must come to grief and result in disappointment and in waste of scare resources, which poor countries can ill afford.

Let me cite one erroneous policy conclusion which has been drawn from the facile, but entirely unrealistic, assumption that there are large masses of unused resources free for the asking and ready to be put to work. This erroneous conclusion occurs again and again in ECLA publications and abounds in Myrdal's writings, and its pernicious influence on policy of many underdeveloped countries must have been strong.

It is said that in underdeveloped countries the restriction of imports by high tariffs, quotas and other measures will not lead to a reduction of the volume of trade, but only to a shift in the composition of imports—from consumer goods (possibly of luxury type) to capital goods. This is in contrast to the developed countries where the classical rule still holds that a restriction of imports leads to a fall in exports and an all round reduction in the volume of trade.

The argument which is often put forward in support of this theory to the effect that poor countries spend all their foreign exchange earnings anyway, and that any dollars they do not spend on those things that are kept out by import restrictions will be spent on something else, is obviously fallacious. It overlooks the fact that the amount of foreign exchange available will be less if resources are drawn into the protected industries away from the export industries. This could be different only if it were true that the protected industries can be staffed wholly or at least to a large extent by workers drawn from the pool of unused resources, i.e., of disguised unemployed rather than by drawing away resources from other industries, including the export industries. This pool of unused resources unfortunately does not exist. The underdeveloped countries are not exempt from the general law of scarcity—they least of all, unfortunately. The theory of disguised unemployment is simply four-dimensional, *deus ex machina* economics—better described as wishful thinking.

Let me emphasize once more that my discounting the idea of disguised unemployment and reducing it to the less exciting and less paradoxical if not trivial and humdrum notion of low, though not uniformly low, productivity in underdeveloped countries, is not meant to add up to a counsel of despair. I do not want to say that nothing can or should be done to raise output and productivity. You will not expect me in three lectures on international trade to give an outline of development policies. There would not be time, and I am not competent for that job. I must confine myself to a few remarks.

I am convinced that the main job has to be done inside each country and that protectionist trade policies can make only a marginal contribution. What needs to be done is to raise gradually the quality of labor by better education, health measures, and the like; to increase mobility, improve the "infrastructure" by investment in public utilities of all description. Probably as much can be done by *removing* social and policy impediments to growth, mobility, private initiative and enterprise, as by positive measures involving large investments.

The third pillar of the theory that free trade always, or at least normally, hinders rather than helps the development of underdeveloped countries, is the assertion that the very fact that the rich countries themselves develop and grow and increase their output and income has, as a rule, "backsetting", i.e., unfavorable effects rather than favorable ones on the poorer countries.

This is indeed a novel view, which flies in the face of classical trade theory. Let me first discuss how the old-fashioned classical economist would argue on this matter. If the industrial countries develop, that is to say, if output and income rises, their import demand for raw material, food, tourist services and goods in general will rise. This, the old-fashioned economist would say, is a clear gain for the less developed countries which sell all those things. (With this conclusion the modern and ultramodern Keynesian economist would heartily agree—for one of his tenets is that the propensity to import is positive, barring the most unlikely case that the majority of imports consist of inferior goods.) The old-fashioned economist will then go on to say that as incomes rise in the developed countries their rate of saving will increase and that there is a good chance that some of the additional capital will become available for investment in less developed countries. This conclusion again will be heartily approved by Keynesians, especially by those who believe in secular stagnation (admittedly a little outmoded now) due to chronic oversaving and lack of investment opportunities in rich countries. Broadly speaking, the conclusion that with increasing wealth in the rich countries more capital becomes available for the poor countries would seem to be borne out by past developments. But it is of course not true that investment opportunities have become less and less in the advanced countries and it is possible that development in the industrial countries may temporarily take such a turn as to absorb a larger proportion of the saving that become available and leave less for export.

By developing and increasing their output, the old industrial countries often deplete their exhaustible resources which gives other countries a chance to export. Britain has practically exhausted her mineral deposits and had to rely more and more on imports from abroad. The U.S., better supplied than the Old World, has been forced to import iron ore from Canada and Venezuela, oil from Venezuela, copper, lead and zinc from Chile, Peru and Africa. Despite occasional setbacks, produced by temporary depressions, protectionist policies and occasionally by discoveries of new mineral deposits or new processes, this development has been proceeding and will undoubtedly continue.

The old-fashioned economist would, of course, readily admit that technological progress in the industrial countries (or for that matter in underdeveloped countries) often is such as to injure particular underdeveloped countries (or particular developed countries). The introduction of synthetic nitrate reduced demand for Chilean natural nitrate, the invention of rayon and nylon was a heavy blow for Japanese silk and to a lesser extent for cotton. The invention of synthetic coffee would be a terrible blow for Brazil and the other coffee countries. But in the meantime Indian textile exports have hurt Lancashire, and Japan's industrial development has stepped on dozens of toes in the older industrial centers.

Admitting all that, or rather stressing it in the first place, the old-fashioned economist, taking a broader view over the last hundred or hundred and fifty years, would nevertheless conclude that the expansion and development of the now comparatively rich countries has been a great boon for the less developed countries, leaving aside the unanswerable question who has gained most. (He would, of course, deny the frequently heard contention that the underdeveloped countries have made no progress at all, being at the same time fully aware of the fact that in some of them a rapid increase in population has swallowed up a larger or smaller part of the rise in aggregate output.) Where would the underdeveloped countries be, and what would their chances of further development be, if they had not at their disposal all the technological and medical improvements, not to mention the purely scientific and "cultural" advances made in the advanced countries? Where would Brazil sell its coffee,

Malaya its tin and rubber, Iraq, Venezuela, etc., their oil—if the developed countries had not sufficiently developed to have effective demand for these things? Where would India sell her textiles and how could other semi-industrialized countries hope to export certain finished goods or export materials more and more in refined rather than raw form, if the highly developed countries did not rapidly develop and pass on from the production and export of the more simple kinds of goods to the production and export of more refined and complicated products, from cotton goods to rayon and nylon, from textiles to machinery, vehicles, pharmaceuticals, and instruments, from simple models to more and more highly fabricated commodities requiring more and more skill, scientific know-how and so on? The old-fashioned economist might go on and ask, as Professor Albert Hirschman has done in his highly challenging and original book *The Strategy of Economic Development*,[36] how could there be any progress at all, for anybody, unless some countries (and individuals) forged ahead of others? Or should we assume that if the advanced countries (or individuals) had not developed as they did, the others would have done it all by themselves? Maybe they would, but how many centuries would have been lost?

These considerations seem to me to establish an overwhelming presumption that the further development of the rise of developed industrial countries will benefit the poorer underdeveloped countries. But let us now consider, against this background, the so-called "backsetting" or "backwashing" effects which the development in the advanced countries is supposed to have on the less advanced, underdeveloped countries.

First it should be recorded that Myrdal does not altogether neglect the favorable effects—the "spread effects" as he calls them. But he pictures them as uncertain and unimportant compared with the "backwash," the unfavorable effects. He makes a molehill out of a mountain and views the problem of how development spreads from the growing points to the surrounding area from an exceedingly narrow and overly static and myopic point of view.

What are, then, the "backsetting," unfavorable effects? It is very difficult to come to grips and find out precisely what these effects are. There is much talk of "interlocking and cumulative causation," of "vicious spirals," and the like. "Suppose that in a community an accidental change" causes "a large part of the population" to lose their jobs. Then the tax rate will go up, "the community will be less tempting for outside business. . . the process gathers momentum . . ." and a "vicious circle" of contraction is set up.[37]

This kind of reasoning is well known from business cycle theory, but the cumulation of an adverse shock into a vicious spiral is essentially a short-run phenomenon and does not upset equilibrium analysis although the new equilibrium, after a disturbance, is usually approached gradually and not established immediately.[38]

Much is also made of the familiar fact (well known to the classical writers as indeed to anyone who has a modicum of historical perspective) that for fairly obvious reasons, the first steps towards economic progress from low levels of development are especially hard.[39]

This may explain why some regions or countries increase for some time their lead over others once they have gotten over the threshold at which growth becomes faster, but it does not explain why that should make it harder for others to do the same, provided the objective (social or physical) conditions there are not less favorable. The few concrete examples of backsetting effects which I have been able to discover are the following:[40] The developing region may attract key personnel from the stagnant region. In other words, a selective migration may start from the poor to the rich country—young, skilled and enterprising people leaving the stagnant area. This cannot be altogether excluded *a priori*, but it is more likely to happen inside a country than between countries. The case of Italy where the North is progressive and the South backward is the standard example. East and West Germany at present is another example—but the political causes are obvious in that case: West Germany enjoys the blessing of a progressive free enterprise system and of liberal democracy, while the economy of the East labors in the stifling atmosphere of an inefficient collectivist system imposed on the country by a dictatorship which is hated and despised by the overwhelming majority of the people. It is at any rate clear that this movement of skilled labor plays at present no important role in the international relationship between the developed and underdeveloped parts of the world wherever we draw—arbitrarily—the line between the two.[41]

The progressive part of a country may also draw capital away from the stagnant part. This again is more likely to happen interregionally than internationally and cannot be an important factor in the relation between the developed and underdeveloped parts of the world.[42] True, there have occasionally occurred capital movements out of underdeveloped countries towards industrial countries (e.g., from Latin America to the U.S. or Europe; but these are instances of capital fleeing from inflation or political dangers as is clearly indicated by the fact that these movements go upstream, as it were, from areas of high to areas of low interest rates. These more or less pathological aberrations do not alter the fact that the *net* capital flows have been on the whole in the right direction, i.e., from the rich to the poor countries.

There remains the vague notion that the developing centers aided by increasing returns due to external economies, will have a "competitive advantage" over the relatively stagnant "peripheral" areas extending over the whole range of industry, leaving to them only primary production where no external economies can be expected.[43]

But these are very extreme assumptions. There exists probably not a single case which fully corresponds to that pattern. The comparative advantage of the developing industrial countries will hardly extend over the *whole* range of industry. Development does not consist exclusively in the reduction of cost of production of existing industries and old products, but largely in the introduction of new commodities and new industries. This is then certain to create gaps in the chain of comparative cost which gives an advantage in certain industrial products to the backward countries. Moreover, external economies often attach to the export sector of the economy even if the exports consist of agricultural products. For example, in the U.S. and Canada the export of agricultural products helped to stimulate the construction of railroads and the opening up of the western part of the North American continent—external economies of gigantic dimensions. Hence less developed countries may benefit from external economies by concentrating on the production of those things where they have a comparative advantage.

I conclude that the argument under consideration can at best justify a certain amount of infant industry protection, but can never invalidate the strong presumption that the rapid growth and development of the rich countries will benefit the poor.

VII.

But I do not wish to spoil my argument by exaggerations. I have promised to make some qualifications and reservations of my free trade position, and I am now ready to do so.

My concessions concern the old-fashioned (one could almost say the "classical") "infant industry argument" for protection. It cannot be denied, I believe, that sometimes well chosen methods of moderate protection of particular industries can help to speed up economic development. This implies that free trade can to some extent retard the development of a country, not compared, of course, with a situation of *no* trade, but compared with a situation in which a certain moderate amount of protection is given to suitably selected industries. There is no presumption at all that the *development* and *growth* of the industrial countries will hurt the less developed countries. My argument that on the contrary, as a rule, the growth of the developed countries will spread to, and benefit, the less developed countries fully stands—although some peculiar constellation is always imaginable in which a particular less developed country (or, of course, developed country) may be hurt by the development of a developed (or underdeveloped country). But this would be in the nature of a fluke and does not invalidate the general presumption of harmony of interests.

Let me now try to state as briefly and as concisely as possible the case for infant industry protection.

It is possible that the development of a particular manufacturing industry, or of manufacturing industries as a whole, will produce "external economies", that is to say, slow pervasive improvements benefiting many or all firms, which eventually will make those industries able to stand up to foreign competition without protection. But since these economies are slow in coming, difficult to foresee, and often of such a nature that private enterprise cannot well appropriate them, private initiative may not be enough to ensure their realization. Let me give what seems to me the most important example: The development of industry in less developed countries is often made difficult or held back by the lack of even moderately well trained, moderately reliable and skilled labor. It is the mistake of the theory of disguised unemployment to overlook, or at any rate divert attention from, this important fact. But untrained, unskilled, unreliable labor can be trained and improved. This improvement is a slow and very costly process. It will usually require force and compulsion, which only the government can wield, to bring it about as quickly as it is desired. But even if its cost, in view of inherent uncertainty, is not such as to put it beyond the power of private business, the private enterprise cannot be sure that the workers, once they have been trained and once the productivity has increased, will not demand the fruits of these improvements for themselves in the form of higher wages. Hence private enterprise cannot always be relied upon to carry out this process, i.e., to produce for a while at a loss in the hope that after labor has become more efficient the enterprise will be able to stand up against foreign competition and recoup the initial losses—or expressed differently, get the rewards for the initial "investment"— investment in skill, training, enterprise.

Now in such a case the government can step in and make the necessary "investment." This can be done either directly in the form of education and training programs or government-operated enterprise, or indirectly: one form of such indirect investment is to grant protection to the industry concerned thus assuring it a market and making it worthwhile to employ workers, even though they are inefficient and costly compared with better paid but more efficient foreign workers. One should not overlook the fact that this policy, even if eventually successful, throws a temporary burden upon the country in the form of higher prices of things that could be obtained cheaper by international trade. But it is the essence of any kind of investment that it causes a temporary hardship. The country foregoes present consumption and welfare in the hope of getting it back in the future. I think it is very important to recognize the operation for what it is—investment of capital, possibly a very profitable investment but involving a temporary burden. The mistake of the theory of disguised unemployment is precisely this;

that it pictures as a free gift of nature what in reality is an act of investment of capital, implying hardship in the form of postponed consumption.

Now capital is scarce and has therefore to be economized. For that reason it is so tremendously important that only worthwhile projects are undertaken. Applied to our case of investment in training, skill, education, by means of import restrictions, it means that a country should protect only those industries which really hold out hope that after a while they will be able to stand on their own feet.

Investment is always a gamble. There is always the danger of misjudging the chances entailing to the loss of all or part of the capital invested. In our case the danger is even greater than usual because the cost is concealed. Private investors, if they do not succeed, are automatically punished. If the private producer does not produce what people want, he will suffer losses. In the case of infant industry protection, the losses of failure are borne by the economy at large in the form of higher prices of commodities that could be provided more cheaply via international trade than by home production. Few people realize what is really going on and hardly anyone is able to figure out the real cost of the operation. Once a new industry has been established behind a high tariff wall it will be very difficult to get rid of the tariff, even if that were possible without endangering the whole industry or a large part of it. There will always be some marginal firms that would really get into trouble, and the other intra-marginal firms will not want to lose the extra profits which protection secures.

It would be nice if it were possible to lay down simple clear-cut criteria which would permit the selection of the industries which are worth protecting and in addition would determine the height of the tariff needed to do the job. I suspect, however, that it will always be necessary to rely on judgment, taking into account the whole structure of the economy and all the measures of internal development policies which are being undertaken at the same time.

I cannot at the end of my lectures even begin to develop systematically my ideas on this matter. Let me simply state in greatest brevity, and hence somewhat dogmatically, my general position.

My preference would be for general measures. I mistrust detailed structural blueprints. These things never work, not even in developed countries where the statistical basis for input-output and similar planning devices is much better than in underdeveloped countries. A uniform import tariff on manufactured goods, or on broad categories of such goods, is probably the best method of infant industry protection. This system leaves the selection of the commodities actually produced to the forces of the market. Especially in countries which are well endowed with entrepreneurial talents this method would be much superior to governmental designation or actual operation of the industries to be developed.

As to the height of the uniform tariff, I would not want to be dogmatic. Let me mention, however, that List himself was of the opinion that an industry that does not grow to maturity with a long-lasting protection of 20–30 percent would not be worth protecting. In other words, it would have to be assumed that the country lacks basic comparative advantage in such an industry.

I am fully aware of the fact that practically all underdeveloped countries (and developed countries for that matter) pursue policies which are almost the exact opposite of those sketched above. They have highly differentiated tariffs and most of them have in addition severe exchange control which is equivalent to high supplementary tariffs, the structure and incidents of which is completely shrouded in administrative secrecy as far as outsiders are concerned, and I strongly suspect are known only in the dimmest outline to those insiders who are in charge of development policies.

It is my contention that this type of policy hurts the underdeveloped countries. In other words, that they could speed up their development by changing over to the system I have sketched. Let me emphasize once more that this advice does not add up to a counsel of extreme *laissez-faire*. It rather means that development policies should be such as to work through and with the help of the powerful forces of the price mechanism instead of opposing and counteracting the market forces. This holds for measures in the area of international trade as well as in the domestic field. I should like to repeat my conviction that the latter—action in the field of education, health, public overhead investment—are more important than the negative policy of import restriction. The latter is, of course, much easier than the former. For that reason, it is likely to be overdone, while the former is apt to be neglected.

THE PIONEER LECTURE:

Liberal and Illiberal Development Policy

Free trade like honesty is still the best policy.
— J. S. Nicholson

I cannot claim to be a pioneer in development economics. But like any economist who is interested in economic policy, I could not avoid thinking and writing about economic growth and development in general. It was then quite natural to apply the general principles of economics to the problems of the developing countries.

Specifically, I came to the problems of development from the theory of international trade. I submit that this is not a bad approach for several reasons. International trade obviously is a

Reprinted from *Pioneers in Development*, Second Series, with permission from the International Bank for Reconstruction and Development/The World Bank.

matter of utmost importance for the developing countries. Just ask yourself how long it would have taken a developing country—Chile, Egypt, Ghana, Mexico, Nigeria, or any other—to reach its present level of development without international trade? It is no exaggeration to say that international trade has been a major factor in the development that has taken place. This is true not only of the now developing countries, but also of the industrial countries in their early stages of development.

Trade provides imports of commodities at lower cost than they could be produced at home, as explained by the static theory of comparative cost; it also provides imports that could not be produced at home. In addition, trade is the vehicle for the importation of capital, know-how, and entrepreneurship. More on all this later.

It is true, however, that if one samples casually the literature on economic development, one might easily get the impression that trade is a most destructive force that locks developing countries in a vicious circle of poverty. The literature abounds with dire predictions of inexorable deteriorations in the terms of trade and pernicious "demonstration effects." There is much talk of massive disguised unemployment in developing countries, which is often misinterpreted as being akin to Keynesian unemployment that is curable by monetary expansion and deficit spending and justifies import restrictions. There are strident denunciations of the monopolistic exploitation of the developing countries by monopoly capitalism this is by no means confined to Marxists and those whom Schumpeter called Marxo-Keynesians.

An extreme example is provided by Gunnar Myrdal. He asserted that "trade operates (as a rule) with a bias in favor of the rich and progressive regions (and countries) and in disfavor to the less developed countries."[1] It is not only that the poor derive less benefit from trade than the rich, but that the poor become poorer if and because the rich get richer. And "by itself free trade would even tend to perpetuate stagnation in the underdeveloped regions" and countries.[2]

Of course, everybody knows that there are situations in which selective trade restrictions can be justified. To put it differently, there exist some widely accepted arguments for tariffs. There is the terms of trade argument that is often called the optimum tariff argument. But the argument most relevant for development economics is the infant industry argument for protection. In fact, the early nineteenth-century proponents of infant industry protection, Alexander Hamilton in the United States and Friedrich List in Germany, can be regarded as early practitioners of development policy.[3] Present-day theorists and practitioners of development economics would do well to familiarize themselves with the literature on infant industry protection, especially with the critical analysis to which the infant industry theory has been subjected by liberal economists such as John Stuart Mill, Frank William Taussig, Alfred Marshall, and others.

Let me make it clear that I use the terms "economic liberalism" and "liberal policy" in the classical nineteenth-century sense of market-oriented, laissez-faire policy and not in the perverted sense that is widespread in the United States and denotes almost the opposite of the classical meaning.

But before going into a more detailed analysis of development economics, I propose to put development economics into historical perspective.

Development Economics and Development Policy in Historical Perspective

The stance of development economics and policies, liberal or illiberal, roughly follows, often with a lag, the stance of general economic theory and policy. This is true even of the development economics of those who claim autonomy for their own brand, "duoeconomics," which says that different economic principles apply to developing and developed countries. In my opinion development economics and development policy should be regarded as part and parcel of general economics and economic policy—more precisely, of growth theory and growth policy. I believe in what some development economists call "monoeconomics"; that is to say, the same economic principles apply to developing and developed countries alike. From the adoption of monoeconomics, however, it does not follow that policy prescriptions should be the same for all countries.

In the fifty or sixty years since development economics has emerged as a branch of economics, a big swing in the general stance of economic policy has occurred. A sharp decline of economic liberalism started with the onset of the Great Depression of the 1930s (or possibly earlier—the precise date does not matter) and reached a low point after World War II. It was followed by a revival of liberalism that started in the late 1940s (the precise date again is unimportant).

The Decline of Liberalism

When "the problems of development were thrust upon economists by the breakup of colonial empires in Asia and Africa during the Second World War and shortly thereafter,"[4] faith in liberalism, in free markets, and in free enterprise was probably at its lowest point since the early nineteenth century. No wonder that the stance of much of development economics, too, was far from liberal.

This is strikingly illustrated by an interesting essay by Raúl Prebisch, one of the most influential development practitioners through his work in the United Nations, in the U.N. Economic Commission for Latin America (ECLA) and the U.N. Conference on Trade and Development (UNCTAD). Prebisch relates that in the 1920s he "was a firm believer in the neoclassical theories." But "the first great crisis of capitalism," the world Depression of the 1930s, had changed his mind. Thus, Prebisch follows Keynes who during the Depression abandoned his early liberal beliefs (see below). But he goes way beyond Keynes when he continues: "The second great crisis of capitalism which we are all suffering now, has strengthened my attitude."[5] What Prebisch here refers to is the world recession of the early 1980s that was caused by the fact that the United States and other industrial countries had to step on the monetary brake to curb inflation. To call this a "great crisis of capitalism" is a gross misinterpretation. Actually, there has been no depression in the post-World War II period, if by depression we mean a decline remotely similar to the Great Depression of the 1930s or earlier ones. Moreover, while Keynes later returned to his early liberal beliefs (see below), Prebisch never found his way back.

The story of the decline of liberalism begins with World War I, 1914–18. This war marked the end, or the beginning of the end, of an epoch—the epoch of liberalism, of relatively free trade, of the gold standard, of free migration, free travel without a passport among most countries (excluding Russia but including the United

States). True, in the 1920s most countries recovered faster from the ravages of the war than had been expected; trade was resumed and the gold standard restored. But tariffs were higher, and new tariff walls were erected in Central Europe between the successor states of the Austro-Hungarian empire. The United States and some other countries had a severe depression in 1920–21, and the countries on the European continent had high and hyper inflation. The recovery lasted barely eight years, 1921–29.

In the United States the Great depression lasted from 1929 to 1933. It was followed by a long recovery, 1933–37, but was interrupted by a short (thirteen months) but extremely vicious depression, and full employment was reached only after the outbreak of World War II in Europe when U.S. rearmament went into high gear.

The worldwide depression was greatly intensified when country after country tried to protect employment by raising tariffs and imposing import quotas and exchange controls. The volume of world trade shrank by about one-third and its value (in terms of gold dollars) by one-half, the difference reflecting the sharp decline in prices of internationally traded commodities.

Hitler came to power in 1933 at about the same time as Roosevelt. Hitler's economic policy was a great success.[6] Unemployment disappeared in a few years, and for several years prices rose little. Thus he was able to give the German people guns and butter at the same time. This greatly strengthened his position in Germany. The U.S.S.R., too, gained economic prestige for two reasons: the immunity of the communist economy to the depression that engulfed the capitalist West and rapid industrialization.[7]

The economic success of the two totalitarian regimes made a deep impression in the West. Along with a fatal misinterpretation of the true nature of the Great depression (see below), it strengthened the tendency among intellectuals, especially in developing countries, to believe in the superiority of controls and central planning over free markets and private enterprise.

The impact of these traumatic events on the stance of economic policy was powerful. For one thing, the Great Depression spawned the "Keynesian revolution" in economic thinking. Whether it really was a scientific revolution is very questionable, but that Keynes was the most influential economist of the century cannot be doubted. True, the main recommendation firmly associated with his name—that if there is much unemployment, the government should engage in deficit spending—was by no means new. If the policy was applied in situations like the one that existed when Keynes wrote his *General Theory*—a situation characterized by high unemployment, declining prices, and deflationary expectations—the policy would have been widely accepted, even by non-Keynesians. But without Keynes's powerful leadership, which called forth scores of devoted and able followers who enthusiastically preached the Keynesian gospel, the New Economics, the policy would not have been put into practice so fast.

Unfortunately, in the post-World War II period Keynesian economists and policymakers applied the policy in situations very different from the Keynesian situation. The postwar environment was characterized by spotty unemployment, rising prices, and inflationary expectations. Thus Keynesian policies had highly inflationary consequences.

Keynes's followers showed little or no concern about inflation. This was, however, not true of the master himself. In 1937, one year after the publication of his *General Theory*, Keynes became concerned about inflation and urged a shift in policy from fighting unemployment to curbing inflation, although at that time inflation was not very high by post-World War II standards and unemployment was still about 11 percent. We have to distinguish between Keynesian economics and the economics of Keynes.[8]

A Fatal Misinterpretation of the Great Depression

The general picture underlying the Keynesian policy prescriptions was that of a "mature" economy that is subject to more or less continual deflationary pressure, chronic oversaving, and a scarcity of investment opportunities because of a slowdown of technological progress. This theory of secular stagnation has been completely discredited by later developments, but it was very popular in the 1930s and was embraced by Keynes in his *General Theory*.

The theory of secular stagnation is a gross misinterpretation of the nature of the Great Depression. Unfortunately, it was taken up by Raul Prebisch and thus had a strong impact on development economics. Actually, the Depression of the 1930s would never have been so severe and lasted so long if the Federal Reserve had not by horrendous policy mistakes of omission and commission caused or permitted the basic money supply to contract by about 30 percent. One need not be an extreme monetarist to recognize that such a contraction of the money supply must have catastrophic consequences. According to Joseph A. Schumpeter, who certainly was not a monetarist but recognized monetary forces when he saw them, the collapse of the U.S. banking system in the early 1930s and the implied contraction of the money supply "turned retreat into rout"; what would have been a recession, perhaps a relatively severe one, became a catastrophic slump.[9] In other words, the Great Depression was not "a crisis of capitalism," as Prebisch says, but was a crisis of largely anticapitalistic government policy, the consequence of horrendous policy mistakes.[10]

Subsequent Developments

That the Great Depression was not due to an inherent, endogenous instability of capitalism as many Keynesians and Prebisch assume, but was the result of exogenous, avoidable policy mistakes, "adventitious factors" as Schumpeter said, is supported by the fact that during the post-World War II period there were recessions, comparatively mild cyclical declines, but nothing resembling the Great Depression of the 1930s or earlier depressions. This was because there was no deflation, no contraction of the money stock.

This favorable outcome had not been foreseen by Keynesian economists. During the war and for years after the war, Keynesian economists predicted that the dismal interwar experience would repeat itself, and that therefore expansionary monetary-fiscal policies were necessary. It stands to reason that this stance of the influential Keynesian economists greatly contributed to the inflationary excesses of the World War II period.

This raises the question of whether we have simply exchanged the horror of deflation for the horror of inflation. Far be it from me to minimize the dangers of inflation, but I submit two points. First, even in highly inflationary countries such as Argentina or Israel, the damage done by inflation has not been nearly so great as the consequences of deflation in the 1930s, measured by loss in output and employment.[11] Second, and more important, to call the recent recession caused by disinflation "the second great crisis of capitalism" as Prebisch does is inappropriate, and the policy conclusions derived from this misinterpretation are ill-advised, to put it mildly.

A medical analogy will make clear what I have in mind. Suppose a doctor has a patient who got himself into serious trouble by living for some time on a starvation diet, but later went on an eating binge. The proper treatment would be to put him on a normal diet and let the recuperative forces of the body do their work. It would clearly be inappropriate to put the patient permanently or for a long time under intensive care, using all sorts of devices to monitor and regulate essential body functions such as heartbeat and breathing. But that is precisely what ECLA and UNCTAD prescribed for the developing countries—all sorts of controls. Prebisch himself probably does not go far in that direction, but his disciples and followers clearly do.

Disintegration of the World Economy

As mentioned above, the Great Depression led to a veritable explosion of protectionism. Under the combined effects of the slump in world output and protectionist measures, world trade fell by about 30 percent in real terms and by 50 percent in nominal terms (gold dollars). The difference reflects the sharp decline in prices of internationally traded commodities. The terms of trade turned sharply against developing countries (exporters of primary products) as they always do in downswings of the business cycle. This was widely misinterpreted as indicating a long-run pattern. It thus led to the famous Prebisch-Singer theory of a secular tendency of the terms of trade of developing countries to worsen—a theory that later research proved to be invalid (see below).

Three interconnected reasons may be roughly distinguished. First, high unemployment made the pressure to protect jobs by shutting out foreign competition almost irresistible. Second, large balance of payments disequilibria were bound to arise, and the prevailing gold standard mentality made it very difficult for deficit countries to relieve deflationary pressures by devaluation of the currency, let alone by floating; therefore, they resorted to import restrictions through quotas and exchange control. Third, free trade conviction among economists, economic journalists, and intellectuals in general had been weakened and protectionist views became fashionable.

To indicate the change in general attitude, it will be well to sketch very briefly Keynes's metamorphosis from a staunch liberal to an all-out protectionist, because he reflected the view of many others and carried along many (though fortunately by no means all) of his followers.

In a famous paper, "National Self-Sufficiency," Keynes wrote: "I was brought up to respect free trade as an economic doctrine which a rational and instructed person could not doubt... As lately as 1923 I was writing that free trade was based on fundamental truths which, stated with their due qualifications, no one can dispute who is capable of understanding the meaning of the words." Ten years later—in 1933—he summed up his views in the well-known passage: "I sympathize with those who would minimize, rather than maximize, economic entanglement among nations. Ideas, knowledge, science, hospitality, travel—these are the things which should of their nature be international. But let goods be homespun whenever it is reasonably and conveniently possible."[12]

When Keynes during the war became involved in planning for post-war economic reconstruction, Bretton Woods, and trade policy, he at first strongly opposed the liberal trade policy proposed by the U.S. State Department. In a memo of October 1943 he wrote: "I am a hopeless skeptic about a return to the 19th century laissez-faire for which the State Department seems to have such a nostalgia. I believe that the future lies with (I) state trading for commodities, (II) international cartels for necessary manufactures, and (III) quantitative import restrictions for non- essential manufactures."[13] Harrod writes: "In the preceding 10 years he [Keynes] had gone far in reconciling himself to a policy of planned trade: these ideas had sunk deeply in. Even for him with . . . his power of quick adaptation, it was difficult to unlearn so much."[14] Another great admirer of

Keynes, Lionel Robbins, wrote: "Even Keynes succumbed to the [then] current insanity... A sad aberration of a noble mind."[15]

Keynes later changed his mind, but many of his followers, notably Nicholas Kaldor and the New Cambridge School, have consistently followed the protectionist line.[16] Kaldor recommends protection of manufactures in Britain and other mature countries to stimulate growth. Unlike agriculture and service industries, manufacturing industries are supposed to enjoy increasing returns to scale hence, protection of manufactures from foreign competition will, it is thought, stimulate growth. Whatever the merits or demerits of a policy of protection for developed countries, it clearly would be highly detrimental for developing countries, especially for the more advanced ones.[17]

Kaldor is wrong when he mentions Germany and France in the late nineteenth century as demonstrating the beneficial effects of protection. In fact, Germany in the crucial years of industrial development had very little protection. The tariff of *Zollverein*, which preceded the establishment of Bismarck's Germany after the Franco-Prussian War of 1870–71, was very low. For the first ten years or so Bismarck continued the low tariff policy of the Zollverein. When he turned protectionist in the late 1870s, the policy was anything but growth promoting. Duties on steel and agriculture, the "Compact of Steel and Rye" as it was dubbed, was inimical to the manufacturing industries.[18]

In his last years Keynes turned sharply against the protection-ist- nationalist policies proposed by his erstwhile followers, who in the meantime had become his critics. It was these policies that he had in mind when he wrote in a famous posthumously published paper: "How much modernist stuff, gone wrong and turned sour and silly, is circulating in our system, also incongruously mixed, it seems, with age-old poison." He pleaded that the "classical medi-cine" should be allowed to work—that is to say, liberal trade policy, convertible currencies, and sound monetary and fiscal policies. "If we reject the medicine from our systems altogether, we may just drift on from expedient to expedient and never get really fit again."[19]

The Changing Tide: The Liberal Revival

The flame of liberalism was sharply dimmed, but never fully extinguished. A tiny flicker was kept alive during the dark days of the Depression by Roosevelt's Secretary of State Cordell Hull, when he initiated the reciprocal trade agreement policy in 1934 and nurtured it into full bloom in the 1940s. After the General Agreement on Tariffs and Trade (GATT) was set up, tariffs were sharply reduced in several rounds of multilateral negotiations.

The reconversion of Keynes to his early liberal beliefs was an important factor in the liberal revival. Keynes's prestige greatly strengthened the liberal cause, and the way in which Keynes's reconversion came about demonstrated the existence of a strong liberal wing among the Keynesians. Keynes's reconversion was largely the result of extensive discussions he had with Roy Harrod, Lionel Robbins, James Meade, Marcus Fleming, and Redvers Opie, when he was working on plans for postwar economic reconstruction.[20]

The liberal resurgence went into high gear in the late 1940s and 1950s when monetary restraints and liberal policies produced economic miracles in several countries. The best known was the German economic miracle which started with the currency reform of 1948 and the simultaneous abolition of all wage, price, and exchange controls by Ludwig Erhard. When the controls inherited from the Nazi period and continued under the military occupation were lifted, the German economy quickly rose from the ashes of the Hitler reich.

Revisiting Early Beliefs

Revisiting early beliefs on development economics turned out to be an exciting and, on the whole, enjoyable task. I was pleased that my main thesis seemed to have stood the test of time very well. In fact, statistical material that has become available and new insights have strengthened the case.

As mentioned earlier, I came to the problems of development from the theory of international trade. My approach has been monoeconomic, as it is often called. In my opinion there is only one economics, neoclassical economics in the broad sense, including the theory of international economic policy. This body of theory is broad and flexible enough to handle the problems of the developing as well as of the developed countries. I reject the idea of duoeconomics, a separate theory for the developing countries. From the monoeconomic approach, however, it does not follow that exactly the same policy recommendations apply for all countries.

I have been critical of the view underlying much of the development economics that developing countries as a group are set apart from the developed countries and are disadvantaged; that they are characterized by heavy "disguised" unemployment; that their terms of trade have an inexorable tendency to deteriorate (the Prebisch-Singer theory); that they are subject to pernicious "demonstration effects"; that private initiative and market forces can be assigned only a minor role; and that development requires "balanced growth" on a large scale and a "big push" brought about through comprehensive "programming" by the government. One of my main objections, expressed in a 1957 paper, was that this approach suffers from what I called "excessive aggregation."[21] I was then referring specifically to the Prebisch-Singer theory of the secular deterioration of developing countries' terms of trade. But it applies to the whole approach.

It is obvious that the developing countries are a very heterogeneous group, even aside from those that form the core of OPEC and float on a third of the world's crude oil reserves. In fact, even the dividing line between developing and developed countries is arbitrary. Different groupings are possible, although all of them are unavoidably somewhat arbitrary, the borderline between the groups being often a little fuzzy. I suggest the following rough classification. First are the economies in East and Southeast Asia—Korea, Malaysia, Taiwan, and Thailand, as well as Hong Kong and Singapore—that are still referred to as "less developed" but are doing quite well. These economies pursue on the whole liberal, market-oriented policies and obviously are not bothered by the handicaps and afflictions mentioned above from which all developing countries are supposed to suffer. Their success is fully explained by, and confirms, the neo-classical paradigm.

The second group includes potentially rich countries that are in financial trouble and suffer from inflation; some are on the verge of defaulting on their foreign debt. To this group belong Argentina, Brazil, Chile, Mexico, Uruguay, and Venezuela.

The outstanding example is Argentina. It is ironic that Raúl Prebisch's country fits so poorly into his scheme of things. Argentina is a potentially very rich country. Years ago Colin Clark in his pioneering study, *Conditions of Economic Progress*, predicted that Argentina would soon reach the level of the United States and Canada. This was not an unreasonable prediction. Argentina is blessed with excellent human and material resources. Its plight has nothing to do with a "crisis of capitalism." It is simply due to horrendous mismanagement that began with the first Peron regime and was continued by successive military and civilian governments.[22]

To the third group belong Bangladesh, India, and Pakistan, where a large part of the world's poor people live. And in the fourth group, sometimes called the "Fourth world," are some very poor and backward countries, mainly in Africa.

The great heterogeneity of the developing countries makes a shambles of any attempt to apply a separate body of economics, development economics, to all of them. It was, however, a great *political* achievement, largely the work of Raúl Prebisch, to bring this disparate group under one umbrella, the caucus of the developing countries. This effective pressure group wields considerable power in the United Nations and other international bodies.

Secular Deterioration of the Terms of Trade

I begin the discussion of the various components of development economics with the Prebisch-Singer hypothesis of the secular deterioration of the developing countries' terms of trade. This was reiterated in Hans Singer's contribution to the first *Pioneers* volume and in a later paper.[23]

I can be very brief because my summary judgement in the 1957 paper that "the alleged historical facts lack proof, their explanation is faulty, the extrapolation [into the future] is reckless and the policy conclusions are irresponsible"[24] has been fully confirmed by later research. I refer especially to Robert E. Lipsey's important book, *Price and Quantity Trends in the Foreign Trade of the United*

States, a study carried out with the careful attention to basic data and statistical methods that one expects in a publication of the National Bureau of Economic Research.[25]

Lipsey reaches the following conclusions: "Two widely held beliefs regarding net barter terms of trade found no confirmation in the data for the United States. One is that there has been a substantial long-term improvement in the terms of trade of developed countries including the United States; the other, that there has been a significant long-term deterioration in the terms of trade of primary as compared to manufacturing products. Although there have been very large swings in U.S. terms of trade since 1879, no long-run trend has emerged. The average level of U.S. terms of trade since World War II has been almost the same as before World War I." During the Great Depression the terms of trade of developing countries deteriorated sharply because primary product prices declined much more than prices of manufactures, as they always did in depressions. The cyclical decline was then misinterpreted as a secular change. Since we now know that there has been no secular deterioration in developing countries' terms of trade, it is no longer necessary to dwell on the alleged causes (Engel's law, business monopolies and union power in the developed countries), which would be inadequate anyway, or to comment on the far-reaching policy conclusions (protectionism, leading to "balanced growth," "big push," and inflation), which must be described as ill-advised, to put it mildly.[26]

To further illustrate the futility of forecasting long-run changes in the terms of trade, I mention a school of thought that was the exact opposite of the Prebisch-Singer doctrine. It held that the terms of trade must inexorably turn against the industrial countries because of the law of diminishing returns in agriculture and in extractive industries. This theory goes back to David Ricardo and earlier writers and had a strange fascination for British economists. Alfred Marshall and J. M. Keynes greatly worried about the British terms of trade. The most extreme position was taken by no less than W. S. Jevons in his gloomy book, *The Coal Question: An Enquiry Concerning the Progress of the Nation and the Probable Exhaustion of the Coal Mines*.[27] In our time Austin Robinson has taken up the theme.[28] It hardly needs lengthy arguing that Ricardo's pessimism and Marshall's and Keynes's worries (not to mention Jevons's forebodings of disaster) have proved entirely groundless.[29]

The Demonstration Effect

Another pillar of development economics is the so-called demonstration effect, from which developing countries are supposed to suffer. I quote from my 1957 paper:

> In our era of improved communication and transportation, of high pressure advertising by means of newspapers, radios, film, etc., consumers in poor countries come into quick and intimate contact with the latest products and gadgets developed and consumed in the richer countries. They try to emulate consumption habits which are beyond their means. This reduces the propensity to save and increases the propensity to import. In the sphere of production the consequence of the demonstration effect is supposed to be that capital intensive and highly mechanized methods of production are adopted which are uneconomical for the resource pattern of the poorer countries.[30]

The demonstration effect clearly is not specifically related to the developing countries. "All of us, even in the most advanced countries, are under pressure by high power advertising to live beyond our means. Everywhere we see and read of things we would like to have and cannot afford. Installment credit makes it easy actually to buy things which we should not buy. Some of us actually are tempted into making foolish purchases, which we later regret; but these slips are quickly corrected and no permanent harm results except if accommodating lax monetary policy leads to inflation."[31] In the early post-World War II period exactly the same reasoning was used in Europe, especially among Keynesian economists, to explain the "permanent" dollar shortage which then was widely supposed to exist. It was, I believe, in that connection that the term "demonstration effect" was first used by James Duesenberry of Harvard University.

The theory of the demonstration effect shows an unbecoming and unjustified patronizing attitude toward the "natives" on the part of development economists from abroad and their disciples in the developing countries. They grossly underestimate the intelligence and responsiveness to price changes of even businessmen in Korea, Malaysia, and elsewhere, let alone the lowly farmers. All that has been convincingly demonstrated by Peter Bauer in numerous writings. While discounting the significance of the demonstration effect in the private sector of the economy, I pointed out that it operates in the area of public policy, the conduct of state enterprises, and the theories that are adopted by the development economists and that underlie their advice to the governments of developing countries.

As I indicated above, when the problems of development were thrust upon the Western world during and immediately after World War II, the faith in free markets and liberal policies was at a low point. The misinterpretation of the nature of the Great Depression and the apparent successes of the totalitarian regimes had made a deep impression on many economists and intellectuals. No wonder that this gave development economics a strong, dirigist, anti-free market, anticapitalist bias.

The most pervasive and damaging example of the demonstration effect is the excessive stress on manufacturing industries and the neglect of agriculture. This has been well described by Harry Johnson in his powerful study, *Economic Policies toward Less Developed Countries*, where he wrote, "Development plans typically steer a disproportionate share of the available. . . resources toward industry . . . Further, development policy . . . depresses [agricultural] incentives [by raising] the price of industrial inputs for agriculture [and by holding] down the prices received by agricultural producers... [Where] an export surplus of agricultural products [exists], it is generally deliberate policy to tax their producers heavily, [reducing] export earning [and encouraging] the development of alternative supplies from elsewhere."[32] Needless to add that protection of agriculture in industrial countries damages the developing countries and pushes them further into protectionism.

A striking and depressing example of the lack of confidence in the efficacy of the price mechanism is provided by the theory of the permanent dollar shortage, which was widely held in the early postwar period. It had a strange fascination for British economists. In a more sophisticated form it was embraced by two giants among economists, J. R. Hicks and D. H. Robertson.[33] The theory is based on faulty theorizing and poor judgment and has been disproved and completely discredited by subsequent developments.

The theory had, however, a strong impact on development economics. It became the theory of the "foreign exchange bottleneck." Developing countries cannot increase their export earnings, it is said, because they are faced with inelastic demand for their products; when they try to export more, the price of their exports declines, so that the value of exports remains the same or even declines.

If this were the rule it would show up in a worsening of the terms of trade. There has been no such long-run deterioration. It is perhaps possible to think of individual cases—banana republics— where something like that may have happened. Banana republics seem indeed to be the model the pessimists have in mind. If there are such cases, they should be identified. But to speak of developing-country or primary-product exporters in general is totally unrealistic.

The theory has been extended and elaborated in many ways. The most important extension probably is the so-called two-gap approach to aid and development. The importance of the two-gap approach is enhanced by the fact that its distinguished author Hollis Chenery for many years held a high position in the World Bank. Chenery and his collaborators argue in many publications that developing countries "typically," although with some notable exceptions, run into intractable bottlenecks, or gaps, which make the economy inflexible and unadjustable. These impediments are intractable in the sense that their elimination cannot be left to market forces; they require government action—in particular, foreign aid to afflicted developing countries.[34]

The two gaps are the savings-investment gap and the import-export gap. the trouble arises from the alleged fact that production functions are often rectangular. To state it in the simplest form, the two factors, capital and labor, cooperate in fixed proportions (rectangular isoquants). The capital-output ratio is assumed to be fixed. Hence, if one factor, say, labor, is in excess supply, there will be unemployment, which can be eliminated only by increasing the supply of capital through more saving, foreign aid, or capital imports. The import-export (balance of payments) gap, or bottleneck, occurs if the targeted growth rate and the necessary investment require inputs imported from abroad, which most developing countries cannot obtain by more exports because foreign demand is inelastic.

All this is, of course, in sharp contrast to the neoclassical paradigm, which postulates variable, not fixed, coefficients and elastic demand. In reply to Bruton, Chenery expresses agreement with most of Bruton's analysis, but he disagrees with the neoclassical assumption of variable coefficients and elastic demand.

In my opinion this is not a realistic model of the development process in the countries currently developing or of the early stages of development in the present industrial countries. What I find the most disturbing are the interventionist implications of the approach and the disdain of the efficacy of market forces. The authorities, both national and international, are supposed to know the appropriate or potential growth rate, the volume of investment required, the supposedly fixed capital- output ratio, and so on. This is a tall order, especially for developing countries whose statistics are notoriously deficient. Furthermore, this approach leads to protectionist conclusions. Since the usual methods of balance of payments adjustment—disinflation, devaluation of the currency, or floating—do not work, in the absence of foreign aid the only way out would be direct controls to cut down the imports of "nonessential" goods in order to make room for the imports of "essential" products. Few economists will accept that conclusion.

The apparent success of the Marshall Plan in helping the wartorn economies of Europe to recover made a deep impression on development economists. It suggested to them that foreign aid is a necessary or even a sufficient condition for rapid development. On several occasions I pointed out that this analogy is invalid, irrespective of one's view of the success of the Marshall Plan.[35] It is one thing to assist the economic reconstruction of a war-ravished industrial country; it is a much more difficult and time-consuming task to help a backward country change its way of life and modernize its economy.

Keynesian Economics and Disguised Unemployment

In my 1957 paper I pointed out that development economists eagerly embraced Keynesian economics and "sadly neglected" what I called "the most serviceable types" of neoclassical economics. These included specifically the neoclassical analysis of the infant industry argument for protection, which is, of course, directly applicable to the developing countries.[36]

The theme has been taken up by Albert Hirschman in his brilliant paper "The Rise and Decline of Development Economics" and echoed by Hans Singer.[37] Hirschman speaks (pp. 375–76) of the "inapplicability of orthodox macroeconomics in underdeveloped areas"; Keynes made the "crucial step" from "monoeconomics" to "duoeconomics." He established the "new economics" applicable to situations with unemployment, which "had instant credibility."

All this is, in my opinion, deeply flawed, confusing, and misleading. To begin with, it is not clearly stated what the orthodox macro policy is that failed in the 1930s and is not applicable to developing countries. It probably refers to the views of those who opposed the Keynesian prescription of deficit spending in a deep depression. That view was widespread in British Treasury circles in the City of London and was held by a small but influential group of conservative economists at the London School of Economics, led by F. A. Hayek, Lionel Robbins, and others (Robbins later changed his mind).

We have seen already that the Keynesian recommendation of deficit spending in an ongoing deflationary spiral is and was shared by many neoclassical economists such as A. C. Pigou and D. H. Robertson, including some monetarists. It did not require a new economics to make this point. For example, it was the prevailing view of Henry Simons, F. H. Knight, Jacob Viner, Lloyd Mints, and others in Chicago that without gross monetary mismanagement the Depression would not have become so deep, but that after a deflationary spiral had been allowed to develop, government deficit spending was in order, preferably through the operation of the automatic stabilizers, to inject money directly into the income stream.[38] As Milton Friedman, Herbert Stein, and others have pointed out, this climate explains why Keynes did not catch on in Chicago as he did in London.[39]

The development economists who embraced Keynesianism failed to distinguish between Keynesian economics and the economics of Keynes. Keynes himself never lost sight of the dangers of inflation. As mentioned above, one year after the publication of his *General Theory*, he urged a shift from fighting unemployment to restraining inflation. Most Keynesian economists, however, have shown little concern about inflation and have continued to urge expansionary policies throughout the post-World War II period.

In my 1957 article I had a lengthy criticism of the theory that there is widespread disguised unemployment in the developing countries, mainly, but by no means exclusively, in rural areas. I pointed out that the concept of disguised unemployment originated in Keynesian circles. Joan Robinson seems to have used the term the first time to designate workers who, having lost well-paid positions in industry to which their skill and training entitle them, are doing odd jobs, raking leaves or selling apples to eke out a miserable living.[40]

In a deep depression, Keynesian unemployment, open or disguised, is easily curable by government deficit spending. This is, of course, not applicable in developing countries. The more sophisticated proponents of this theory, W. A. Lewis, Ragnar Nurkse, and P. N. Rosenstein-Rodan, recognize this, but they insist that at least in the more densely populated countries of Asia and Africa disguised unemployment is heavy in rural areas.[41] That means that a fraction of the labor force—25 percent is often mentioned—could be withdrawn without a loss of output. In other words, the marginal productivity of labor is zero or even negative.

Although this situation is not inconceivable in isolated cases, I have strong doubts that it ever existed anywhere on a considerable scale. I have pointed out that the idea of disguised unemployment is associated with the proposition that the capital-labor ratio is fixed; in other words, that the isoquants in the production function are rectangular (or at least angular). I have also demonstrated that the theory of disguised unemployment can be regarded as an extreme and unrealistic version of the theory that in many developing countries, and perhaps in some developed countries too, the quality of labor in agriculture is lower than that in industry; in other words, that agriculture is a backward sector of the economy.

There surely is some truth in this assertion. The process of development will lift backward areas to higher levels through investment in material capital as well as in human capital. There is, of course, much room for public policies to speed up the process of development—for example, by providing better infrastructure and better education.[42] But to speak of disguised unemployment because workers will produce more when better tools, machines, and education become available is totally inappropriate. In that case, everyone is a disguised unemployed, because in the future we will all produce more with better methods of production, better tools, and better education.

Naturally I was very pleased when I discovered that Jacob Viner and Theodore W. Schultz strongly reject the theory. In a well-known article, Some Reflections on the Concept of "Disguised Unemployment,"[43] Viner has this to say:

> As far as agriculture is concerned, I find it impossible to conceive of a farm of any kind on which, other factors of production being held constant in quantity, and even in form as well, it would not be possible, by known methods, to obtain some addition to the crop by using additional labor in more careful selection and planting of the seed, more intensive weeding, cultivation, thinning, and mulching, more painstaking harvesting, gleaning, and clearing of the crop. I am not aware that anyone has ever given a convincing illustration of a technical coefficient, which is "fixed" in any valid economic sense. [Speaking of the steel industry, he says:] If iron ore, or coal, were as expensive per ton as gold I am sure that the steel industry would find ways of appreciably reducing the amounts of iron ore, or of coal, it uses to produce a tone of steel of given specific character, even though the chemical constituency of the steel were invariant, and, moreover, it would readily find ways of changing the chemical constituency of a ton of "steel" without reducing its suitability for its ordinary uses, and this

not only in the long run but in the very short run.

Nobel Laureate Theodore Schultz is just as emphatic as Viner in rejecting the theory of widespread disguised unemployment. He is doubly qualified as a renowned expert on world agriculture and for his seminal work on human capital. He quotes approvingly Viner's statement concerning agriculture cited above, and he sums up his views as follows "The conclusion with respect to the doctrine that a part of the labor working in agriculture in poor countries has a marginal productivity of zero is that it is a false doctrine. It has roots that make it suspect. It rests on shaky theoretical presumptions. It fails to win any support when put to a critical test in analyzing effects upon agricultural production of the deaths in the agricultural labor force caused by the influenza epidemic of 1918–1919 in India."[44]

Trade Policies for Developing Countries

I always took it for granted that neoclassical trade theory, as developed by Viner, Heckscher, Ohlin, Meade, Samuelson, or myself is applicable for both developing and developed countries. It never occurred to me that a different theory applies to developing countries. The thesis of duoeconomics came later. Traditional trade theory includes, of course, the theory of trade policy which is a branch of welfare economics. Most trade theorists lean toward free trade, but all of them realize that there exist exceptions to the free trade rule. In view of the great diversity of developing countries, the theory of duoeconomics makes no sense. Why should a different theory apply to Argentina and Australia, or to Brazil, Portugal, and Spain?

The classical theory of comparative cost in its modern form presents a greatly simplified model of general equilibrium which lends itself to diagrammatic analysis. It has proved a versatile tool of analysis. Much has been made of the fact that the basic model of comparative cost, like most general equilibrium theories, is static and assumes perfect competition. Development problems, however, are essentially dynamic in nature; therefore, it is argued, a static theory is of no use. But the argument is fallacious. Although the simplest theory of demand and supply is static, nobody would doubt that it is applicable to developing countries.

In my Cairo lectures, I argued at some length that the static nature of trade theory does not deprive it of usefulness in exploring dynamic processes.[45] There is, after all, the method of comparative statics. True, for certain problems, such as the short-run business cycle, comparative statics is of little use. But the trade problem is different. Static gains from trade along the lines of comparative cost enable a country to save and invest more. Furthermore, it attracts capital from abroad and fosters the importation of technical know-how. This means that the static production possibility curve is pushed out. I recalled that classical and neoclassical theorists were fully aware of the dynamic effects of trade. John Stuart Mill, for example, argued at great length that in addition to the direct (static) beneficial effects of an international division of labor according to comparative costs, trade has powerful indirect (dynamic) effects by "placing human beings in contact with persons dissimilar to themselves, and with modes of thought and action unlike those with which they are familiar." This is "principally applicable to [countries in] an early stage of industrial advancement," that is, to what we now call developing countries. According to Mill, "indirect benefits of commerce, economical and moral, [are] still greater than the direct."[46]

I now come to the main question what is the proper trade policy for developing countries? Most developing countries pursue highly protectionist policies, which are often called—euphemistically—a policy of import substitution, especially with respect to manufacturing industries. In many cases the results have not been good. The economic landscape in some developing countries is littered and disfigured by white elephants, modern factories unsuited to their productive resources, which either stand idle or operate inefficiently at exorbitant costs, with protection from imports or direct subsidies at the expense of the taxpayer and the traditional export sector—mainly agriculture. The demonstration effect at its worst. Tanzania is a sad example.

Terms of trade Argument for Protection. The terms of trade argument comes in two different versions, a static and a dynamic one—the latter applicable specifically to developing countries. The static version, also called the optimum tariff theory, is beloved by trade theorists because it lends itself to elegant mathematical and diagrammatic analysis. It states that any country or group of countries that is confronted with foreign demand for its products with an elasticity of less than infinite can improve its position by imposing restrictions on imports or exports, a duty whose height depends on the elasticity of foreign demand. In other words, any country that, unlike the individual wheat or dairy farmer, is not confronted with infinitely elastic demand for all its products wield some monopoly power which it can exploit in a variety of ways.

The theory has been elaborated in many different ways. But it is not necessary to go into details, for it seems clear that there exists not a single developing country that has any control over its terms of trade. This is more true now than it was earlier because of the tremendous growth of the world economy and of world trade since World War II and the emergence of new industrial centers in many parts of the world, including the Third World and the communist bloc.

This development has made the world economy more competitive than it was and has also made obsolete a theory that was popular among the development economists in the early post-World War II period. This theory holds that the developing countries are confronted by monopolistic markets in their purchases of manufactured goods, and that prices are kept above competitive levels by international private cartels or simply by the absence of price competition among producers operating in imperfect markets.[47] In the early years after World War II, U.S. industry had a quasi monopoly because Europe, Japan, and the communist countries lay prostrate from the ravages of war. But the world economy has completely changed since then. Moreover, even if it were true that developing countries are victims of monopolistic exploitation on the import side, it would not follow that their proper response should be protectionist measures. On the contrary, this response would make things worse.

In the past, many attempts have been made to organize international cartels and collective restriction schemes for rubber, tin, coffee, and the like. All these attempts have failed. The only successful one—for a time—was OPEC. But even mighty OPEC is now in disarray. The mills of markets grind slowly but powerfully. After some delay, OPEC's monopoly power was undermined by market forces when the high price of crude oil stimulated conservation of energy and induced a successful search for oil outside the OPEC countries.

To sum up, the static terms of trade argument for protection simply does not hold any more, if it ever did. The dynamic version is based on the Prebisch-Singer thesis that the terms of trade of developing countries have a secular tendency to deteriorate. If this were true it could be argued that protection of manufacturing simply speeds up an unavoidable development. But since the Prebisch-Singer thesis is invalid, it cannot supply an argument for protection.

The arguments for protection that appear relevant for developing countries are the infant industry, unemployment, and external economies arguments. These arguments are indeed interrelated.

Infant Industry Argument. In what might be called a synthetic picture of views widely held by supporters of infant industry protection and development economists, I will try to make the case for protection as reasonable as I can.

Unemployment is in the center of the stage. The most reasonable interpretation of the alleged existence of heavy rural unemployment in developing countries is not that the marginal productivity of labor is literally zero, but that the efficiency of labor in agriculture is low, perhaps very low, compared with that of agricultural labor in more highly developed countries and also with that of labor in industry in the developing countries themselves. The lack of an efficient, educated, disciplined labor force is, of course, a great handicap for the development of industries. But inefficient labor can be trained on the job. This is, after all, what happens in the process of development. The crucial question then is, can and should the process be speeded up by providing support to industry through restraints on imports or in some other way—or should it be left to market forces?

I present two answers to this question: first, the view of the proponents of infant industry protection which is shared by many development economists and, second, that of classical free traders.

Infant industry protection is, to use modern terminology, largely investment in human capital. To make it possible for nascent industries to provide on-the-job training for inefficient and therefore expensive labor, they need "temporary protection" from foreign competitors who are not handicapped by inefficient labor. This applies not only to workers, but also to managers and possibly fledgling entrepreneurs.

Free trade economists, of course, argue that free markets will take care of the problem. Peter Bauer recently restated his view in a powerful article, "Myths of Subsidized Manufacturing."[48] He flatly calls the infant industry argument invalid. "Business people are prepared to finance the early stages of an activity they expect will become viable. Indeed, they routinely do so in manufacturing, trade, transport, and commercial agriculture alike."

For a different view, I first quote a free trader, John Stuart Mill, who says in his *Principles*: "But it cannot be expected that individuals at their own risk, or rather to their certain loss, will introduce a new manufacture, and bear the burdens of carrying it on until the producers have been educated to the [efficient] level."[49]

Mill did not say why he thought that this was not to be expected. An attempt to give a precise reason came much later. What I have in mind is Paul N. Rosenstein-Rodan's theory of the "inappropriability" of labor skills. He explains it this way: "Under a system of slavery it paid the owner to invest in training a slave because the increase in skills would benefit the investor. When slavery was abolished, a worker trained could contract with an outside employer who did not have to bear the cost of his training. Whoever invested in the training of the worker would run the risk of not being able to appropriate the benefit of increased productivity. The training and education of workers under competitive market conditions would therefore be below optimum. This is a widespread phenomenon." In other words, in a free country "there are no mortgages on workers."[50]

There may be some truth in all this, but it surely requires further analysis. The theory must assume that there are institutional rigidities and distortions. For in a fully competitive economy, where factors of production are remunerated according to their marginal productivity, untrained labor would receive a correspondingly low wage. That would mean that the cost of training would be borne by the trainees, not by the trainers. Hence, there would be no presumption of underinvestment. Thus the Rosenstein-Rodan effect would not materialize.

True, it can be argued that in many developing countries, just as in industrial countries, wages have become rigid, union power has increased, and government policies have fostered this development through welfare measures, minimum wages, and so forth. Such policies, which in some industrial countries took fifty years or longer to develop, were adopted in some developing countries in a hurry.

But this does not justify import restrictions. In fact, such restrictions are a poor second or third choice. The first choice is clearly to change the policies that cause the rigidities and distortions. The theory can and has been elaborated in many different ways. For example, Robert Lipsey has suggested to me that Gary Becker's distinction between general and specific training can be usefully applied. Becker defines the two types of training as follows:

> General training is useful in many firms besides those providing it: . . . firms would provide general training only if they did not have to pay any of the costs. Persons receiving general training would be willing to pay these costs since training raises their future wages. Hence it is the trainees, not the firms, who would bear the cost of general training and benefit from the return . . . Completely specific training can be defined as training that has no effect on the productivity of trainees that would be useful in other firms. . . If all training were completely specific, the wage that an employee could get elsewhere would be independent of the amount of training he had received . . . The wage paid by firms would also be independent of training. If so, firms would have to pay training costs, for no rational employee would pay for training that did not benefit him. Firms would collect the returns from such training in the form of larger profits resulting from higher productivity.[51]

The general conclusion to be drawn from this analysis would

seem to be that a good deal of the costs of on-the-job training can be left to competitive markets, but there surely is a case for public expenditure on education to foster general training.

External Economies and Diseconomies. The problem of external economies plays a great role in development economics.[52] The concept of external economies was first introduced by Alfred Marshall in his *Principles*. It can be defined as influences that flow from the expansion or contraction of one firm or industry to other firms or industries, and that for one reason or another are insufficiently acknowledged by the market or not acknowledged at all— nonmarket interactions for short. Neoclassical writers, for example Jacob Viner, distinguish between technological and pecuniary external economies.

It is easier to think of examples of technological diseconomies than of technological economies. This has become clear in our age of environmental concern. Pollution of air and water are real problems that are dealt with by administrative and legislative actions. Development economists tend to neglect diseconomies when they assert that external economies are more important in industry than in agriculture. This is hardly true of diseconomies.

Tibor Scitovsky defines pecuniary external economies as follow: If industry A invests and expands, it is bound to have pecuniary repercussions on any or all of the following industries: (1) on industries which produce intermediate goods (such as machinery and materials) used by A; (2) through cheapening of A's own products, on industries which use A's products as intermediate goods; (3) on industries on whose products factors used in A spend their additional income; (4) on industries whose product is complementary in use to the product of A.[53] To repeat, according to neoclassical writers these interindustry reactions are not really external; they are reflected in price changes, and market participants take them into account. Development economists such as Rosenstein-Rodan, Scitovsky, and others, however, assert that in the "dynamic context of development these pecuniary external economies become real." Scitovsky puts it this way: "In the market economy prices are the signaling device that informs each person of other people's economic decisions and thus guides production and investment decisions. Market prices, however, reflect the economic situation as it is and not as it will be. For this reason they are more useful for coordinating current production decisions . . . than . . . for coordinating investment decisions, which have delayed effects . . . and should be governed . . . by what the future economic situation is expected to be . . . Hence the belief that there is need either for centralized investment planning or some additional communication system to supplement the pricing system as a signaling device."[54]

In my opinion this analysis misunderstands the working of a dynamic decentralized market economy. It ignores the role of the entrepreneur and underestimates his capability to foresee the consequences of his action. Of course, any investment carries a certain amount of risk. The larger the investment and the more durable the equipment, the larger the risk. But any adaptation to a change carries uncertainty and risk. The distinction between current production and investment is one of degree. It is therefore misleading to say that the equilibrium theory applies only to the former.

Rosenstein-Rodan and Scitovsky have been quite consistent in their policy conclusion. As Scitovsky puts it, to capture the alleged pecuniary external economies, of which the private producers are supposed to be unaware, simultaneous expansion of all industries is necessary. Only complete integration of all industries can do the job.[55] This amounts to a plea for comprehensive central planning.

Using different language, Rosenstein-Rodan reaches the same conclusions. He pleads for a "big push," that is to say, simultaneous expansion of many industries. For good measure he also urges a large investment of social overhead capital by the government to provide an elaborate infrastructure and calls for government programming of the process of economic development; this too amounts to a call for central planning.

Providing a good infrastructure—education, law and order, a good monetary system, and so on—is, of course, vitally important for economic development, and in many developing countries these public services badly need improvement. But when the call for massive expenditures on infrastructure comes on top of a big push to expand many industries through government actions at public expense, the whole program becomes a recipe for economic disaster. It would greatly overburden the weak administrative capabilities of developing countries, overtax their economies, and open the floodgate for corrosive inflation.

The best policy would be to let free markets, in other words, capitalism, do what they do best—develop new industries. Direct investment by foreign corporations should be encouraged, because they provide technological know-how and on-the-job training. Unfortunately, one often finds that foreign companies are denied permission to set up branches in developing countries because this would make life harder for the protected state enterprises. This is development policy at its worst.

As indicated earlier, these theories were developed after the Great Depression and during or immediately after World War II, when faith in free markets was at an all-time low and the prestige of the two totalitarian regimes, Nazism and Bolshevism, and their alleged economic successes were at their zenith. Since then the situation has completely changed. We are now in a position to compare the performance of market economies and centrally planned ones: the German Democratic Republic and the Federal Republic of Germany, the Democratic Republic of Korea and the Republic of Korea, Austria and Cechoslovakia, Greece and Yugoslavia; pairs of countries with similar backgrounds that in the past have enjoyed the same standards of living. Other examples are Taiwan and China, Malaysia and Thailand versus Burma. There can be no doubt that market economies have performed better.

There surely are cases where judicious, temporary restrictions on imports can be justified to help infant industries. For markets are often imperfect, and private investors make mistakes. But market failures and mistakes in the private sector usually correct themselves, possibly in a recession. The business cycle is still with us. In the past fifty years enormous technological advances in transport, communications, and information have made markets much more competitive than they were at the time when new development theories emerged.

Faulty government policies, however, are hard to change. When controls do not yield the intended results, the controls are not abolished but tightened; when the response to a policy of subsidies is not what was expected, the subsidies are raised and the policy continues and infant industry protection is likely to be extended to senility. As Deepak Lal, in his hard-hitting classic, wisely remarked: "Imperfect markets [are] superior to imperfect planning."[56]

Exchange Rate Policies for Developing Countries

Many developing countries suffer from high rates of inflation. If that is the case they should let their currencies float to minimize the adverse effects of inflation on their foreign trade. They should avoid import restrictions for balance of payments reasons, and avoid exchange controls like the plague.

The best policy would be to curb inflation sufficiently to make it possible to peg the currency to a suitable foreign currency, to special drawing rights (SDRs), or some other basket of currencies—but of course they must make sure that the currency is fully convertible into the currency or currencies to which it is pegged without the use of controls.[57] According to statistics of the International Monetary Fund, thirty-four countries peg their currencies to the dollar, thirteen African countries peg to the French franc, eleven to SDRs, and so on.

Proposals have been made, especially in Latin America, to organize regional monetary unions, analogous to the European Monetary System (EMS). In my opinion, this is not a good approach. A monetary union requires very tight coordination of monetary policy, which is almost impossible to achieve by sovereign states. The example of the EMS is misleading for two reasons: first, the EMS is, after all, backed up by the European Community; second, despite the impressive facade, the EMS has not been an outstanding success from the economic point of view.

Excessive Pessimism

Most of the development literature, both private and official, is imbued with deep pessimism about past performances and prospects for the future of the developing countries. To some extent this pessimism may be regarded as a negotiating stance; for much of the literature, even the unofficial literature, is meant to support demands of the poor countries for foreign aid and other concessions from the rich industrial countries. Whatever the motive, in my opinion, the pessimism is unjustified.

To set the record straight, I can do no better than to quote the world's foremost authority on economic growth, Simon Kuznets. In his magisterial lecture, "Two Centuries of Economic Growth: Reflections on U.S. Experience," Kuznets summed up the results of the enormous amount of research that he and others have done in recent years: "Even in this recent twenty-five year period of greater strain and danger, the growth in peacetime product per capita in the United States was still at a high rate; and in the rest of the world, developed and less developed (but excepting the few countries and periods marked by internal conflicts and political breakdown), material returns have grown, per capita, at a rate higher than ever observed in the past."[58]

In his paper, "Aspects of Post-World War II Growth in Less Developed Countries," Kuznets had this to say: "For the LDCs as a group, the United Nations has estimated annual growth of total and per capita GDP (gross domestic product at constant factor prices) from 1950 to 1972. The growth rate of per capita product . . . for the twenty-two years was 2.61 percent per year . . . Such growth rates are quite high in the long-term historical perspective of both the LDCs and the current DCs. These high growth rates are largely a recent phenomenon, the result of the post-World War II period of comparative liberalism and liberalization."[59]

Kuznets is, of course, fully aware of the dangers of using broad aggregate measures of growth for the developing countries as a group, given the great diversity among them. He discusses and carefully evaluates possible biases in the procedures. But after everything has been said and done, he stands by the basic soundness of his findings and is puzzled that, despite the "impressively high" growth rates "in the per capita product of LDCs over almost a quarter of a century," the general sentiment in the developing countries is one of dissatisfaction and gloom that "seems to ignore the growth achievements." He conjectures, and gives ample reasons for this conjecture, that "a rise in expectations has produced a negative reaction to economic attainments which otherwise might have elicited litanies of praise for economic miracles."[60]

I suggest three factors that have aroused excessively optimistic expectations. The first one is that the early economic success of the U.S.S.R.—rapid industrialization and growth, and immunity from the depression that engulfed the West in the 1930s—made a deep impression in the developing as well as in the developed countries. It engendered the belief that through comprehensive central planning governments have it in their power to lift backward countries, in one great leap, to a higher level of development. It took a long time for the persistent conspicuous lag of the centrally planned countries behind the market economies to shake confidence in the superiority of central planning. This issue cannot be further discussed here. I confine myself to asking a simple question: How is one to explain the glaring gap in the per capita GNP and standard of living between such pairs of countries as the German Democratic Republic and the Federal Republic of Germany, Austria and Czechoslovakia, Yugoslavia and Greece—pairs of countries that enjoyed about the same standard of living in the pre-communist era?

The second factor to arouse over-optimistic expectations was the apparent success of the Marshall Plan in speeding European recovery after the war. We have seen that the analogy of the Marshall Plan and foreign aid to developing countries is invalid.

The third factor was the great success of the oil cartel in lifting the standard of living in most member countries of OPEC. But mighty OPEC countries have recently fallen on hard times. The high price of crude oil has stimulated conservation of energy and the search for alternative sources. The demand for OPEC oil has sharply declined. The mills of the market often grind slowly, but they always grind powerfully.

Comment

W. Max Corden

Gottfried Haberler is not a development economist as this term is usually understood. He has not written about particular developing countries—that is, currently low-income countries—nor has he focused primarily on their specific problems. But his work is actually highly relevant, both to the analysis of their own policies and to the impact of world macroeconomic developments on these countries. Indirectly, his contributions to trade theory have probably had a greater effect on their policies and the analysis of their policies than the work of some of the development pioneers presented in the first volume in this series.

Above all, Haberler is one of the great figures of international economics in this century.[1] He played a crucial role in the construction of the modern pure theory of international trade by introducing the opportunity cost approach (which replaced the confusing real cost approach espoused particularly by Viner). This new approach clarified the nature of the gains from trade and the law of comparative advantage and went beyond Ricardo's special constant cost case.

With further contributions from Lerner, Leontief, and Samuelson (on the gains from trade), and then from Samuelson (incorporating the great Heckscher-Ohlin insights), the foundations of modern pure trade theory were laid. In addition, Haberler's classic textbook, *The Theory of International Trade*, written in his early thirties, has laid the foundation for much later work. It sorted out (and usually demolished) many arguments for protection. It foreshadowed various models and ideas that became prominent later, such as the specific factors model of trade theory.

Most important for the analysis of economic policy of developing countries is his modestly titled but actually quite revolutionary article, "Some Problems in the Pure Theory of International Trade,"[2] which initiated the theory of domestic distortions. In this article he analyzed the implications for the gains from trade of a number of domestic distortions, notably externalities and factor price rigidities. Perhaps his main contribution was to show that immobilities of factors of production (factor specificity being an extreme case) do not affect the case for free trade, but that factor price rigidities do. This pioneering work was subsequently expanded to the analysis of protection and to the consideration of various other cases by Meade, Johnson, Bhagwati, and others. It has been very influential and, in effect, led to a reconstruction of the theory of trade policy.

Gottfried Haberler made his international reputation with *Prosperity and Depression*, first published in 1937 and revised four times after that, the last in 1964.[3] This book critically analyzed numerous pre-Keynesian trade cycle theories, displaying an unsurpassed mastery of the extensive literature in this field and an ability to consolidate and integrate. The later editions took account of Keynes's contributions. Above all, this book showed historical perspective and detachment, something for which Keynes and his followers were not noted. It also foreshadowed numerous ideas that became more prominent later. The book was a *tour de force* and an immediate success, receiving enthusiastic reviews. Subsequently Haberler has written extensively, but in a less integrative fashion, on domestic and international macroeconomic issues, particularly on the international monetary system and (skeptically) on various reform proposals.

His paper here speaks for itself. It is utterly clear, written in Haberler's usual simple, unpretentious style. It certainly does not require summarizing. What comes through is his historical sense, his constant awareness of the contributions of earlier scholars, and his breadth of approach. A good part of it might be regarded as rather negative, because he reviews his criticisms over the years of a whole range of questionable arguments that were temporarily fashionable. For this reason I have drawn attention to his important positive contributions. In my view he has been consistently correct; one reason being that his arguments are always carefully qualified, a characteristic to which I shall return. Many of the criticisms he made seem obvious today, but it is worth noting that Haberler was *right at the time*, not afterwards. As a discussant of his paper I suffer from the serious disability that I agree with him almost entirely and know of no way of saying better what he has already said so straightforwardly. No doubt criticisms can be made from points of view with which I have little sympathy. To me it seems hard for a reasonable person to disagree.

A common strand in some of the arguments that Haberler has criticized over the years is a tendency to draw long-term conclusions from short-term events. Haberler has always seen the folly of this *at the time*. The Great Depression, from which the world was slow to recover, in the later 1930s led to the theory of secular stagnation, which was still being written about after World War II. The current account surplus of the United States in the immediate postwar period, combined with the physical shortages in Europe which were obviously the result of war-time dislocation and destruction, led to the theory of the *long-term* dollar shortage. The decline in the terms of trade of commodity exporters in the Depression, and again after the Korean boom, led to elaborate theories claiming that there was a long-term tendency for the terms of trade of developing countries to decline. The conclusion I draw from this is that one should be hesitant to draw conclusions about long-term trends from developments that may be short-term. In fact, it is hard if not impossible to detect such trends, if indeed there are any, from the observation of recent and brief periods.

If one wished to criticize Haberler's paper, perhaps one should note that Scitovsky would no longer agree with his 1954 argument (about pecuniary externalities) that private decisionmakers use only existing and past prices as guides to resource allocation and ignore expectations; this leads to rather simple-minded conclusions about the need for centralized coordination. I also find it hard to believe that Gunnar Myrdal in the 1970s stood by his beliefs of the 1950s quoted by Haberler.

In addition, Haberler's remarks about the irrelevance of the terms of trade argument for trade restrictions for developing countries seem to be too sweeping. In fact, his lack of caution here is uncharacteristic, and qualifications need to be pointed out. After all, the OPEC cartel did succeed in improving the terms of trade of its members for a considerable time. The gains are being gradually eroded, so that it is impossible to sustain the conclusions derived from purely static theory that there is some firm, permanent, optimal degree of trade restrictions. But there have been terms of trade gains in that particular case. One could find other cases in which temporary—but significant—gains are likely to have been obtained from some degree of trade restrictions. This does not mean that trade restrictions should be greater than they now are, but rather that the national optimum may sometimes justify some modest degree of restrictions. But this is a rather minor quibble. An empirical judgment is involved, and one might argue that the OPEC case is *sui generis*. If, as is usual, the potential gains concern an improvement in export prices, the optimal policy requires export taxes or cartels, not import tariffs or quotas. Other than in a two-good model, tariffs and quotas cannot be "symmetrical" (à la Lerner) with an optimal structure of export taxes, a structure that is likely to be nonuniform.

Haberler notes that in the postwar period there has been nothing resembling the Great Depression because there were no substantial deflations through sudden money contractions. He notes that this favorable outcome was not foreseen by Keynesian economists. It might be said that there were no severe deflations *because* Keynesian policies were being followed, so that the only fault of the Keynesians was in failing to foresee the successful adoption of their messages.

This raises the deeper question of why depressions were avoided after World War II and why, until 1973, remarkably low levels of unemployment were maintained in all the developed countries. Was this really the result of Keynesian policies? For one thing, until the so-called new economics came to the United States, Keynesian theories were explicitly accepted in only a limited number of industrial countries, notably Britain and other Commonwealth countries and Scandinavia. The United States, Germany, and France were not explicitly Keynesian. Even in the "Keynesian countries" investment demand was buoyant and relatively stable, so that there was no great need for countercyclical fiscal stabilization policies. But one could argue that in those cases the knowledge that Keynesian stabilization policies would be followed if needed (and were followed to a modest extent) helped to generate the stability and buoyancy of investment.

I would add another explanation of the long-term tendency for all the industrial countries to have little unemployment until the early 1970s, whether or not they professed to follow, or actually did follow, Keynesian policies. The explanation involves a mixture of neoclassical theory and historical or sociological factors. Workers—more specifically, trade unions—were willing to accept real wage levels which were compatible with full employment, a willingness that was gradually eroded in the 1970s. This moderation in real wage demands and expectations was explained by the memories of the Depression and, in continental Europe, of the earlier inflations and the hard times of the immediate postwar period. Furthermore, underlying growth rates were so high (partly *because* of wage moderation) that for a long time expectations of living increases did not get ahead of the increases that were actually possible at full employment levels.

If the real wage levels had *not* been accepted by trade unions, nominal wages would have increased further and, with monetary expansion, would have squeezed profits and thus generated unemployment. Given the fixed exchange rate system and the stable monetary policies being following in the United States, further monetary expansion would have created balance of payments problems outside the United States, as occasionally it did. If this were avoided with exchange rate depreciation, eventually the inflationary consequences would have led to restrictive measures and thus to unemployment.

All this is a somewhat lengthy diversion provoked by some brief remarks of Gottfried Haberler's. To return to the main subject, something must be said about Haberler's style or approach. It does not appeal to those who like drama or flamboyance. Some might argue that if ideas are to make an impact they must be stated in extreme form. Haberler, however, is too scholarly, has too much knowledge of and respect for the contributions of scholars of earlier times, and is too aware of the qualifications to most simple propositions to engage in the sort of bold generalizations or statements, and spurious claims to originality, which are often found effective for maximum impact.

Haberler's early skepticism about Keynes's contributions is well known, and I have found particularly interesting his sympathetic but similarly skeptical remarks about the most recent development in macroeconomic theory: rational expectations. His few pages on the subject at a conference in 1980, where he criticized the "hardline version" of this theory—a type of criticism that five years later is perhaps conventional—are instructive.[4] He agrees that countries should not "fine-tune," but also believes that they should *not* rule out discretionary anticyclical policy when there is a serious recession. The Keynesian prescription (one not merely advocated by or owed to Keynes) *was* appropriate for the 1930s. Turning to rational expectations, Haberler queries the sharp distinction between "systematic" or predictable policies and "unsystematic" policies on which the theory focuses and from which some early contributors derived some rather far-fetched conclusions. Furthermore, he points out that not all agents in a market appraise policies in the same way, and not everybody is a monetarist. He prefers the "post-Keynesian consensus," whereby expansionary monetary and fiscal policies can have significant real effects, even when announced in advance, but effects on inflationary expectations must also be taken into account. Haberler is thus no macroeconomic extremist. And all these issues concern developing countries. The new developments in macroeconomic theory have been applied to developing countries, mainly in Latin America, and they have affected and will continue to affect the thinking of domestic policymakers and domestic and foreign advisers.

In the first volume of this series Paul Streeten suggested some thought-provoking categorizations for development economists. I have been wondering where Gottfried Haberler fits in.

Is he a constructionist or a skeptic? Obviously, he is a constructionist about the uses of the neoclassical model. He uses it continuously, and he shows, for example, that static models are useful even in a dynamic world and that, in any case, the theory does not ignore dynamics. (Quite early, in his well-known *Survey of International Trade Theory*,[5] however, he called for improvements in a dynamic direction, a call that has, in fact, been heeded by subsequent contributors to trade theory.) He is a constructionist when he refutes silly arguments against trade theory, which take simple heuristic models (such as Samuelson's factor price equalization model) literally and criticize trade theory because one cannot observe results that appear to follow from very simple models. With his continual and sensible use of neoclassical theory he is indeed an archconstructionist. But Haberler is, of course, also a skeptic, not only about the numerous unsound generalizations and confused arguments to which he refers in his paper, but also about more recent extreme arguments on the neoclassical side, namely (as I have mentioned) the theory of rational expectations.

Is Haberler a utopian or a pedant? He is definitely not a pedant. Indeed, pedantry irritates him, and he has never been fond of excessive formal theorizing (note his skeptical references to the elaborations of the terms of trade argument for protection). At the same time, his style is certainly nonutopian. He is too much of a skeptic and too judicious. But, in a sense, he *is* a utopian, while recognizing the short-term costs that may be involved in getting to Utopia. He does believe that a system of free markets and free trade (subject, I need hardly add, to some qualifications) is the most efficient way of organizing an economy, and he has consistently advocated moving in that direction. Although he does not suggest that Utopia would result, he has no doubt that great improvements could, in many cases, be brought about by moving in that direction. And, in a manner of speaking, the Utopias—or at least the role models—do exist, though never, of course, perfect.

In referring to Argentina, Haberler used the phrase "horrendous mismanagement." No doubt this could be used about the economic policies of many other countries, although Argentina may have given the world some of the most dramatic examples. Indeed, in many countries at many times there is "horrendous mismanagement," and economists like Haberler spend their time preaching against it and hoping to improve things with their preaching. In a sense, we are all management consultants, often not too successful in our advocacy, but always optimistic that we can do some good, this being a particular form of utopianism. But this raises the thought that there is more in heaven and earth than horrendous or wise management. There are larger issues on which Haberler has not touched but which are relevant to the issues he discusses.

To some extent, politicians and political behavior are endogenous, reacting to pressure groups and reflecting deep-seated historical attitudes. Thus, a belief in planning and regulating when there are economic problems, and in restricting imports when a local industry is in trouble, comes naturally to people all over the world. The extent of these beliefs depends, among other things, on collective memories of earlier events, especially crises, as well as on ideologies that may have originated far back in history. Politicians who engage in horrendous mismanagement rarely see themselves as free agents, and the question is to what extent economists can actually affect events by clarifying issues and explaining consequences. Clearly, the varying impact of economic advice and preaching and the explanation of why horrendous policies were actually followed are important matters for study but somewhat outside the tradition in which Haberler has been writing.

Gottfried Haberler has been a "liberal" economist—defined in the continental European sense—all his life. He has believed in free markets and free trade and has been unsympathetic to interventionist policies. For many years, notably in the late 1930s, these views were not in fashion. After World War II they came back into fashion in Germany and to some extent in the United States, but they were quite out of tune with the conventional wisdom of the new field of development economics. In the 1970s the advantages of the market system, the need for liberalization, and an awareness of the excessive costs of import substitution in developing countries came to be widely, though not universally, accepted by students of developing countries and practitioners of development economics.

I need not go into details here, since this is so well known. Various writings, such as those by Ian Little, Tibor Scitovsky, and Maurice Scott,[6] played a role, but possibly even more important were the success stories of the outward-looking newly industrializing economies, notably Korea and Taiwan. In effect, Haberler was a precursor, who kept the free market or liberalization flame alight. Now, when one rereads him, one finds much that is obvious, quite moderate, and close to the mainstream. In assessing him, one should assess the whole of this school of thought and its battles with the protectionists.

There must really be two aspects to this assessment. First, there is the purely analytical aspect. The "nonorthodox" have always been weak analytically. Haberler and the many followers in mainstream neoclassical economics have provided the analytical framework. They have successfully destroyed many of the protectionist arguments that have been used (for example, the argument that *if* the terms of trade were moving against developing countries this would provide an argument for protection); in other cases, they have demonstrated the rigorous conditions required for the arguments for protection to be correct.

Second, there is the question of whether the free marketers are making the right empirical judgments when they imply that the qualifications to the free trade arguments are relatively unimportant and when they give more weight to the likelihood of government or bureaucratic failure than to market failure. Here views are much influenced by the country that people have in mind. It is worth stressing that for large economies, notably China and India, freeing domestic markets may be relatively more important than opening up to the world market, although the two openings are likely to be connected.

There is never a clear choice between imperfect markets and imperfect planning. Even in the most regulated societies some markets do operate, and in countries with the freest markets there are elements of planning, both in the public sector—inevitable in the provision of public infrastructure—and within corporations. There is always a continuum. But it is certainly a widely accepted view, which I share, that in most developing countries the bias has been too much toward interventionism. This leads sometimes to an

imperfect attempt at planning and more often to a highly un-
planned response to the interests of special pressure groups. A shift
in the free market direction is certainly desirable.

Haberler has clearly been much influenced by the success of
relatively free market policies in European countries, notably
Germany under Erhard, and the contrast with Eastern Europe
hardly needs laboring. He has not, to my knowledge, written
specifically about the experiences of countries that are currently
developing or low-income. But followers of his point of view have
been much influenced by the experiences of a limited number of
countries, principally in East Asia. They do not usually suggest
(and I suspect Haberler would not) that a removal of restrictions
and an outward-looking approach would unhesitatingly and universally ensure development and economic dynamism. There can
be many factors holding back development. But a reasonable
degree of liberalization, although not sufficient, is surely in most
cases a necessary condition for real progress.

Comment

Ronald Findlay

Nineteen hundred is not only the title of a film by Bernardo Bertolucci. It was also the year in which Gottfried Haberler was born. He has therefore lived through every year of our turbulent and exciting century. His paper is no mere academic disquisition but a reflection of events and ideas that have shaped the evolution of the world economy and the very texture of the lives we lead within it.

The grand theme around which Haberler organizes his exposition is the fate of liberalism as an economic doctrine in the twentieth century. The Great Depression of the 1930s, which he sees as a massive aberration rather than some inherent "structural contradiction" of the capitalist system, gave rise in his view to the pernicious influence of Keynes, not only in the short-term economic management of the advanced industrial economies but also in the longer-term development policies adopted by the newly independent countries of the Third World. In common with other distinguished economists of Austrian or Austro-Hungarian persuasion, such as F. A. Hayek and William Fellner, he traces the roots of inflation and macroeconomic instability in the West to the intellectual deficiencies of naive Keynesianism. These are reflected in the once popular notion that the so-called Phillips curve offered policymakers a "menu of social choice" in which they could secure full employment at some fixed rate of inflation. The reasoning behind this was shattered by the work of Milton Friedman and my colleague Edmund Phelps in the late 1960s.

Haberler, however, does not stop here. He traces the Keynesian infection to development policy in the developing countries as well—chiefly, it seems, on the ground that the concept of disguised unemployment stems from that most eminent of left-wing Keynesians, the late Joan Robinson. Disguised unemployment is also seen as a justification for state intervention to plan for industrialization on the basis of a strategy of import substitution. Thus one huge error leads to another, and development theory and policy are seen as having led to decades of misfortune in Latin America, India, and other parts of the developing world.

Just as he sees the troubles of earlier postwar decades, in both the developed and developing worlds, as being the consequence of Keynesian heresies, he sees the past few years, with Reagan and Thatcher, as marking a return to sanity and the free market. Freed from the hubris of Keynesian activism, the West can provide the basis for a stable and prosperous world economy, in which the developing countries can join on the basis of free trade and capital movements to steadily raise their per capita incomes.

I personally share Haberler's commitment to liberalism in trade and development policy, so I am in general agreement with his criticism of much of conventional thinking about development and the emphasis on planning and state intervention associated with it. Like him, I "come to the problem of development from the theory of international trade," and like him I consider that an advantage (perhaps even an absolute and sound one!) and not a hindrance; like him I see no contradiction between rapid and sound development and international specialization on the basis of comparative advantage. I do, however, respectfully disagree with him on several of the nuances, both of the intellectual history of the development theory and the experience of the past few decades with development. I hope that many disagreements are based mainly on misunderstanding, owing to the fact that he is obviously forced by the limits of space to paint with a very broad brush and has therefore perhaps not been able to qualify and modulate his statements as much as he would have wished.

· My comments are in three parts. The first notes the points on which I feel the need to modify the views expressed by Haberler in his paper. The second looks at the standard neoclassical theory of international trade, on which he has been one of the major influences, in relation to some of the main concerns in the field of economic development. The final section looks at some perennial problems of the trade and development literature that have drawn continued attention from Haberler: the infant industry argument and the secular tendency of the terms of trade between advanced and developing countries.

I.

Whatever one thinks of the logical consistency or empirical relevance of the concept of disguised unemployment in the development theory of the 1940s and 1950s as expounded by Paul Rosenstein-Rodan, Ragnar Nurkse, and Arthur Lewis, there do not seem to me to be any plausible direct links to Keynesian unemployment—that is, unemployment caused by a deficiency of aggregate demand. All of the development writers traced the problem to a basic deficiency of the *supply* of complementary inputs, such as arable land and physical capital, relative to the population and potential labor force, and not to a deficiency of aggregate *demand* à la Keynes.

They also did not claim any "free lunch" on the basis of the diagnosis of disguised unemployment. It was recognized that effective utilization of this "hidden potential" would raise demands for the limited supply of food from the countryside. This in turn would give rise to the familiar "scissor's crisis" of the U.S.S.R. in the 1920s, involving the terms of trade between town and country that figured prominently in the early development literature. The dilemma of the planners in charge of urban industry was whether to induce a flow of food to the towns by supplying plentiful consumer goods in return, or to opt for heavy industry in the subsequent Stalinist pattern of the early five-year plans in the 1930s.

The terms of trade between town and country when the urban industrial sector is controlled by the planners while the rural sector is populated by an independent peasantry was much discussed in the development literature of the 1960s by such writers as Maurice Dobb and A. K. Sen, in addition to W. A. Lewis and others.[1] This literature, even in the case of Marxists such as Dobb, did focus on the key role of relative prices and was often based on impeccable neoclassical principles of demand and supply. Indeed, the theory of international trade, Haberler's own specialty, is fully applicable to this problem. The notion of "primitive socialist accumulation," put forward by the Russian theorist Eugene Preobrazhensky, could be interpreted as the application of an optimum tariff by monopolistic urban industry against competitive rural agriculture; the maximized profits would be plowed back into capital accumulation in industry to serve as the driving force of the system over time.

The problem with much of this literature was that it assumed that neither town nor country in the developing economy was connected to the outside world. This was a realistic assumption for Russian writers such as Preobrazhensky and Feldman but was quite unjustified for almost any developing country after World War II. The well-known Indian statistician, P. C. Mahalanobis, formulated his very influential methodology of Indian planning on the basis of a two-sector model that completely ignored foreign trade, so that the only possibility of growth was to allocate investment to the domestic capital goods industry. This was somewhat modified by K. N. Raj and A. K. Sen,[2] but they *assumed* that export earnings were stagnant and therefore came to the same policy prescriptions as Mahalnobis. The justification for this assumption was that India's traditional exports, such as tea and jute, faced very inelastic world demands, and no attention was given to the possibility of labor-intensive manufactured exports despite India's long experience in this field. This missed opportunity was of course fully exploited a little later by the East Asian economies. The "foreign exchange gap" approach, associated with the work of Hollis Chenery, also made this ultrapessimistic assumption. Considering the extent to which India tended to dominate development thinking, and the sanctity that numerically quantified but behaviorally crude models tended to enjoy, it is perhaps not surprising that the opportunities for outward-looking development were ignored by so many for so long.

Thus, while I tend to share Haberler's critical view of much of the development literature of the 1950s, I trace the basic problem to the distrust of international trade as an engine of growth and not to any direct or indirect influence of Keynesian ideas. What lies behind *both* explanations, of course, is the devastating effect of the Great Depression of the 1930s, which destroyed the faith of almost an entire generation not only in the benefits of free trade but also in the working of the price mechanism itself. Like Ragnar Nurkse in particular, development economists tended to look back to the 1870–1914 era as a golden age of expansion that was based on free trade and capital mobility and would never be restored. Ironically, this was just when world trade was beginning to undergo a rate of expansion that made anything in that era pale into insignificance.

Alterations in relative prices were regarded as undesirable and potentially disruptive to economic health and order, and that is why balanced growth was advocated—that is, increasing supplies in line with income elasticities of demand through conscious planning. The belief in the possibility of massive disguised unemployment, at least in some countries, could also be seen as necessitated by the acute pessimism regarding foreign trade. The mobilization of the underemployed domestic labor was a substitute for the neglected external option.

Another point on which I believe I have a significant difference of opinion with Haberler is his characterization of the East Asian "gang of four" as economies which "pursue on the whole liberal, market-oriented policies" and whose "success is fully explained by, and confirms the neoclassical paradigm." No one doubts the extraordinary success in recent decades of these economies, and that it has been done by taking full advantage of the opportunities opened up by an expanding world economy. Only in the case of the British colony of Hong Kong, however, has something close to laissez-faire been practiced. In the case of the others there is extensive intervention and promotion in the form of state enterprises, subsidies, regulations, and other measures affecting the capital market, domestic savings, the trade regime, and indeed almost every aspect of the economy. I find it difficult to consider Korea, Taiwan, and Singapore "liberal" societies in the classical sense of the word as Haberler uses it, when the state intervenes so heavily not only in the economy but in the private lives of their citizens. It is true that state intervention in these economies has a complementary rather than restrictive or tutelary relationship to the private sector, as in India, for example, but it seems inappropriate to characterize their polices as "liberal" in the true sense of the word.

II.

The literature on development is replete with criticisms of the theory of comparative advantage, most of which were usually flagrant errors based on the most elementary misunderstandings. Non sequiturs, in particular, abound. Many years ago even so distinguished an economist as Thomas (Lord) Balogh made a long list of the assumptions usually found in textbook demonstrations of the theory of comparative advantage.[3] He had no difficulty in demonstrating that most of these assumptions did not hold in the real world. He triumphantly concluded that he had totally demolished the theory. It was left to Haberler to explain patiently the difference between necessary and sufficient conditions and to show how the "gains from trade" proposition was valid even in the complete absence of familiar assumptions such as perfect internal factor mobility.[4] His paper on this subject has become a classic, and its major role in the subsequent literature on distortions developed by J. N. Bhagwati and V. K. Ramaswami and others is very well brought out in an essay in commemoration of Haberler's eightieth birthday by Robert Baldwin, one of the most eminent of his students.[5]

As Haberler has noted again here, one continues to hear the canard that trade theory is "static," while development is "dynamic," so that the former is of no relevance to the latter. Once again a non sequitur and once again Haberler has to point it out gently but firmly. He does not, however, go further and mention that the dynamic extension of trade theory that he himself called for in his *Survey of International Trade Theory*[6] has now largely been accomplished, and it gives no more comfort to protectionists than the traditional static doctrine does.

As is well known, both Haberler's "opportunity cost" doctrine of comparative advantage and the Heckscher-Ohlin theory in its formal representation by Samuelson and others were based on fixed supplies of the factors of production, including not only raw labor and natural resources, but also physical and human capital. Since both types of capital are man-made and functions of economic variables that are themselves functions of the volume and pattern of trade, it is essential for a theory of international trade to account for them endogenously. This has been done in the past twenty years by integrating neoclassical growth theory with international trade theory, along lines first rigorously established by H. Oniki and H. Uzawa.[7] As I have pointed out, it is possible to distinguish between "momentary" and long-run" comparative advantage.[8] The first is based on the per capita capital stocks at any particular instant, and the second on the steady-state values of these levels, as determined by parameters such as propensities to save and rates of labor force growth.

One of the most famous ideas of the Austrian School, of which Haberler is a luminous representative, is its view of the role of time in the three grounds for a positive rate of interest first expounded by Bohm-Bawerk. I have drawn on this Austro-Wicksellian tradition in an attempt to place the Heckscher-Ohlin approach to trade on a more fundamental microeconomic basis.[9] Here it is the country that is more "patient," in the sense of discounting the future at a lower rate, and that ultimately has a comparative advantage in the more capital-intensive or roundabout processes of production. Thus there is no need to postulate arbitrarily given stocks of capital or even saving propensities in the Keynesian fashion but only individual tastes with regard to present and future consumption.

Education is an obviously Austrian production process, since there must be a waiting period between the input of resources, such as teaching, and the emergence of output in the form of skilled labor. The incentive to acquire education obviously depends on the differential between the wage rates of skilled and unskilled labor. According to the Stolper-Samuelson theorem, this differential depends on trade itself, and so we need a model that can *simultaneously* handle trade and the formation of human capital in an intertemporal framework. This has only recently been done.[10]

With a perfect capital market there is no case for any state intervention in these models. The free trade solution is the first-best, except for the optimum tariff argument, which always applies when there is monopoly power in trade, even in the traditional models. It is true, however, that free trade could *reduce* the formation of skills and human capital, for example, by narrowing the wage differential of skilled labor as a result of obtaining skill-intensive goods more cheaply through imports. This is not an argument for protection, however, since a better result could be obtained by free trade together with an education subsidy, although even this would result in less national welfare than free trade.

Policies that aim to increase physical or human capital formation can change long-run comparative advantage in the sense defined earlier. At any instant, however, it is always best to allocate the available resources efficiently, and that means following free trade. Nor does it follow that policies that raise steady-state welfare as a result of protection are better than free trade, since it is necessary to compare not only steady-state welfare levels but also the entire integral of welfare, including the time spent in reaching the higher steady state, which is when the cost is paid in terms of forgone consumption.

Another source of possible justification for irrational economic policies in developing countries comes from a misapplication of the theory of the second-best. The contention here is that since the free market in developing countries is beset by all sorts of pre-existing distortions of one kind or another, it makes no sense to apply any sort of rational calculus along neoclassical lines to any new projects or measures. A variant of this argument is that even if such a calculus were possible in principle, the relevant shadow prices would be so difficult to determine that it could not be made.

A fundamental contribution by I. M. D. Little and J. A. Mirrlees, however, has shown that there is no basis for such a nihilistic position.[11] The relevant shadow prices are simply the world market prices, in the case of tradable goods, for an economy without monopoly power in international markets. This is true in the case of most developing countries for most tradable goods, and where there is monopoly power the relevant shadow price is the marginal revenue (for exports) or marginal cost (for imports). The shadow prices for primary factors and nontraded goods can then be derived in principle from the world prices of the tradable goods.[12] The costs and benefits of new projects, direct foreign investment, migration of labor, royalties for new technology, and so on can be evaluated at these prices. Thus even in the presence of distortions that are regarded as irremovable, the world market imposes a rational discipline on the allocation of resources. The best alternative, of course, would be to remove the distortions altogether, but it is important to realize that it is *not* the case that there is no alternative to perfection in the neoclassical approach.

III.

Two central ideas in the field of trade and development have been the infant industry argument for protection and the alleged tendency for a secular deterioration in the terms of trade of the developing countries. The first of these of course goes back to Hamilton and List, while the second appeared around 1950 in the independent work of Raúl Prebisch and Hans Singer. Haberler has always given the first idea a fair and sympathetic hearing, but he has been severe in his strictures on the logical basis and empirical accuracy of the latter. As he points out here, his early skepticism has been abundantly confirmed by subsequent research. In view of the attention that Haberler has given to these doctrines in all his writings on trade and development, it would be appropriate to close my comments with some observations on each of them.

It is now generally recognized that there is a logical case for infant industry protection on the basis of the "learning by doing" argument; that is, productivity improves as a function of the cumulative volume of output, as in the well-known article of Kenneth J. Arrow.[13] The production process produces not just the good itself but also more skill in the work force, which has a social value and therefore a positive shadow price that a perfectly competitive firm cannot capture. An output subsidy, *not* an import tariff, is therefore warranted, the level of which has to be adjusted to equate the private with the social return to firms in the competitive industry where this effect occurs. P. K. Bardhan has worked out an intertemporal model with an optimally varying subsidy of this sort.[14] Other arguments for infant industry protection usually involve inperfections in the capital market or the market for skilled labor, and so are best dealt with by direct action in those markets.[15]

All these issues are by now very well understood. More interesting and controversial is what may be called the "infant exporter" argument: is there a first-best case for export subsidies? This problem gains much of its interest from the related issue of export-oriented development strategy of the type that seems to have been pursued by at least some economies in East Asia. There is considerable confusion in the literature as to exactly what is meant by "export orientation" in a trade regime or development strategy. According to one interpretation it simply means restoration of neutrality in the incentives to produce exportables, importables, and nontraded goods. Korea and Taiwan, for example, and quite heavily protective import substitution strategies in the 1950s before they began their outward orientation in the early 1960s. Since the original protection has been lowered only gradually, and in fact still exists in many sectors, the incentives for exporters, such as remission of duties on imported raw materials for export production, were in the nature of countervailing measures. I am not aware of precise calculations which show whether these measures fell short of, exactly offset, or overcompensated for the initial bias against imports.

As argued by Paul Streeten and myself,[16] and as I am sure Haberler would agree, the basic neoclassical doctrine would be as critical of net export subsidies as of net import tariffs, since welfare is maximized at the point at which the marginal rate of transformation between exportables and importables is equal to the ratio of world prices. It can be argued, however, that there is a marketing technology for exporting that has to be learned. Thus a learning by doing argument can be applied to the activity of exporting instead of to the activity of production. Again an externality is involved that cannot! e captured by competitive firms, so there is a first-best case for an export subsidy, as worked out very neatly by Wolfgang Mayer.[17]

Prebisch's views on trade and development contain at least three separate strands and arguments that are often confused. One is the assertion, on the basis of sketchy data for Britain's terms of trade from 1870 to 1940 by the German historian Werner Schlote, that there was a historical secular deterioration of the terms of trade of the developing countries as a whole. This assertion has been overwhelmingly rejected by the weight of subsequent empirical research and criticism, with Haberler as one of the earliest and most acute critics.

Second is the contention that laissez-faire with competitive markets will drive exports in developing countries to the point at which marginal costs is equal to price, but above marginal revenue because of unexploited monopoly power. If such monopoly power exists, then of course the familiar optimum tariff argument applies and the case is granted in principle. The extent to which such power exists at the national level is vigorously disputed here by Haberler, and cartels at the international level present their own familiar problems.

Prebisch presented a loose but very perceptive and insightful informal model of the interaction over time between the growth of an advanced industrial "center" and a primary producing "periphery," in which the movement of the terms of trade appeared as the result of trends in technical progress in the two regimes, mediated by differences in market structure and in parameters such as the income elasticities of demand for imports. His view was that monopolistic labor and goods markets in the center retained the fruits of technical progress in manufacturing, while in the periphery atomistic competition resulted in these gains being dissipated by losses in the terms of trade. His center-periphery model was therefore characterized by an asymmetry in structure between the two regions.

The neoclassical analysis of the terms of trade between growing economies emerged slightly larger, with J. P. Hicks and H. G. Johnson as the pioneers.[18] A modern analytical synthesis between the Prebisch center-periphery model and the neoclassical approach has recently emerged in a number of what are called North-South models.[19] In my model the South specializes in primary products (or labor-intensive manufactures) and the North in manufactures (including capital goods). The South has a dual labor market à la W. A. Lewis, and the North has an exogenously growing labor force that is always fully employed a la R. M. Solow.[20] The terms of trade emerge as the regulator of the growth rate of the South, deteriorating when it grows faster and improving when it grows slower than the North. A steady-state value of the terms of trade would maintain equilibrium between the two regions. A number of unorthodox implications can be derived from this and similar models.

The work of Arghiri Emmanuel and also Lewis has recently shifted the focus of attention from the commodity or barter terms of trade, which is the relative price of commodities, to the so-called double factoral terms of trade, which is the rate of exchange between the labor of the trading countries.[21] The unequal character of exhange would presumably be removed if the double factoral terms of trade were equal to unity; that is, the products of one man-year of labor in the North exchange for the products of one man-year of labor in the South. With wage rates higher in the North than in the South this condition will not hold, and so the North "exploits" the South within this view of the problem.

If this is the way people choose to define terms, then the conclusion follows and there is no point in arguing further. However, the definition has peculiar consequences that may not make it so attractive for its proponents. Thus suppose that country A and country B exchange one unit of cloth for one unit of steel, with a unit of labor producing one unit of cloth in A and one unit of steel in B. Then there is no unequal exchange and everything is apparently as it should be. Suppose, however, that a unit of labor in country C can produce three units of steel, and C is willing to give country A two units of steel per unit of cloth. In exchange for its cloth export country A can thus get twice as much from C as from B, but A would become a "victim" of unequal exchange if it accepted the doubly more favorable offer!

A genuinely just order for world trade, consistent with even such widely divergent ideologies as Marxism and classical liberalism, would seem to be one which permitted the free mobility of labor across national boundaries.[22] Accepting this proposition seems to me to be the acid test for the liberal philosophy that Haberler has so eloquently espoused in all his writings.

NOTES

1. "The Theory of Comparative Costs and Its Use in the Defense of Free Trade," *Weltwirtschaftliches Archiv*, 32:349-370 (1930 II). Translated from German. Reprinted in *Selected Essays of Gottfried Haberler*, edited by Anthony Y. C. Koo (Cambridge, Mass.: M.I.T. Press, 1985), pp. 3–20.

2. "International Trade and Economic Development," *National Bank of Egypt Fiftieth Anniversary Commemoration Lectures* (Cairo, Egypt: National Bank of Egypt, 1959), reprinted in *Selected Essays of Gottfried Haberler*, pp.495–527. "International Trade and Economic Development" is reprinted in this volume and referred to as the Cairo lectures. I have discussed some of the problems of economic development in two earlier papers: Gottfried Haberler, "Terms of Trade and Economic Development," in *Economic Development for Latin America*, Howard Ellis and H. C. Wallich, eds. (New York, N.Y.: St. Martin's Press, 1961), reprinted in *Selected Essays of Gottfried Haberler*, and Gottfried Haberler, "Critical Observation on Some Current Notions in the Theory of Economic Development," *L'industria*, No. 2 (Milan, Italy, 1957). The 1957 essay is essentially an abbreviated version of the Cairo lectures.

   Also reprinted in this volume is "Liberal and Illiberal Development Policy," in *Pioneers in Development*, Second Series, Gerald Meier, ed., published for the World Bank (New York, N.Y.: Oxford University Press, 1987), pp. 49–103.

3. On the relation between classical and neoclassical trade theory, see my paper "Survey of Circumstances Affecting the Location of Production and International Trade as Analyzed in the Theoretical Literature" in *The International Allocation of*

Economic Activity, Proceedings of Nobel Symposium (Stockholm, Sweden: Bertil Ohlin, 1977), reprinted in *Selected Essays of Gottfried Haberler*, pp. 109–32.

4. Published for the World Bank by the Oxford University Press, New York. For a brief summary see the article "Industrialization and Foreign Trade" by Sarath Rajapatirana in *Finance & Development*, September 1987, a quarterly publication of the International Monetary Fund and the World Bank.

5. See his "The Communist Manifesto in Sociology and Economics" in *Essays of Schumpeter*, edited by Richard V. Clemence (Cambridge, Mass.: Addison-Wesley Press, Inc., 1951), p. 293, reprinted from the *Journal of Political Economy*, June 1949, pp. 199–212.

6. A memorial volume in honor of Rául Prebisch has been published by the Research Centre for Cooperation with Developing Countries, Ljubljana, Yugoslavia, "Homage to Rául Prebisch" in *Development & South-South Cooperation*, Vol. 2, No. 3, December 1986, 207 pages.

7. See Rául Prebisch, "Five Stages in My Thinking on Development," in *Pioneers in Development*, Gerald Meier and Dudley Sears, eds. (New York, N.Y.: Oxford University Press, 1984), p. 175.

8. Recently Prabirjit Sarkar in his paper "The Prebisch-Singer Thesis of Terms of Trade Deterioration: Some Doubtful Questions vis-a-vis Recent Findings" (See Prebisch memorial volume, pp. 123–36) has tried to defend the Prebisch-Singer theory against its critics. Sarkar's paper presents a very useful bibliography of the huge literature on the Prebisch-Singer hypothesis. But he does not take into account Bela Balassa's convincing criticism of Hans Singer's 1984 attempt to buttress his theory with arguments and statistical sources similar to those used by Sarkar. See *Pioneers in Development*, pp. 304–11.

9. Peter Bauer, *Dissent on Development*, 2nd edition (Cambridge, Mass.: Harvard University Press, 1976), p. 38 ff.

10. Keynes's articles in *The Times* are reprinted in T. W. Hutchison, *Keynes versus the "Keynesians". . .?: An Essay in the Thinking of J. M. Keynes and the Accuracy of Its Interpretation of His Followers* (London, England: Institute of Economic Affairs,

1979) and in *The Collected Writings of J. M. Keynes*, Vol. XXI (Cambridge, England: Cambridge University Press, 1979).

11. Theodore W. Schultz, *Transforming Traditional Agriculture* (New York, N.Y.: Arno Press, 1976), p. 70.

12. For references see my *Pioneers* lecture.

13. Ravi Batra, *The Great Depression of 1990* (Dallas, Tex.: Venus Books, 1985) and Stephen Marris, *Deficits and the Dollar: The World Economy at Risk*, updated edition (Washington, D.C.: Institute for International Economics, 1987).

14. "The Great Depression of the 1930s—Can It Happen Again?" included in *The Business Cycle and Public Policy, 1920–80, A Compendium of Papers* submitted to the Joint Economic Committee, Congress of the United States, November 28, 1980, and reprinted in *Selected Essays of Gottfried Haberler*, pp. 405–27.

Cairo Lectures

1. English edition, Princeton, New Jersey, U.S.A., 1949, p. 286.

2. Needless to add that the growth of "tertiary" industries is a sign or symptom of development only when it comes "naturally". One cannot turn the argument around and assume that if the Government puts a large part of the people into tertiary occupations, say entertainment or even dentistry by artificial means, it will automatically raise the level of economic development correspondingly.

3. Physical output may be lower than in some less developed countries owing to comparatively poor soil and climate. Value output may still be high, if import restrictions keep the price of agricultural products high.

4. Fear of blockade in case of war or fear of being at the mercy of unfriendly powers is, however, not so easy to dispel.

5. Germany did have some colonies before the first World War. But I don't think that any economist would argue that they were economically speaking of any consequence.

6. Needless to add that statistical problems of measurement remain. What I am speaking of is theoretical criteria.

7. It also goes without saying that in countries where the Government runs the economy—in the communist countries—it has

also to conduct foreign trade. But socialist state trading, if it is efficient and rational and motivated by economic objectives, would be along the lines of comparative cost. I might add that socialist theoreticians fully agree to that, although many do deny that trade in capitalist countries is, in fact, conducted along these lines.

8. In many cases very expensive and poor substitutes can be produced. There is not much sense in contemplating extreme situations. But if I were pressed to guess, I would say that the developed countries as a group, and a few of them individually, could get along without trade a little easier (although still at a terrific loss) than the underdeveloped countries.

9. William: "The Theory of International Trade Reconsidered," *Economic Journal*, 1929. Myrdal: *Development and Underdevelopment*, National Bank of Egypt, 1956.

10. It is strange that Myrdal, who quotes copiously from earlier and contemporary writers (see especially the full dress presentation of his views in *The International Economy*, New York, 1956) fails to mention List, to whose theory his own bears a most striking similarity, notwithstanding the fact that List's policy recommendations are more moderate than Myrdal's.

11. The short run business cycle, on the other hand, is a type of problem of which a static explanation is rather useless. That is the reason why the *static* Keynesian system is so barren. In the short run, dynamic factors completely overshadow and distort the static Keynesian relationships—especially the liquidity preference and the investment function. Needless to add there are plenty of so-called "Keynesian type" dynamic models. But logically they have very little to do with the static Keynesian theory and nothing at all with the chapter on the "Trade Cycle: in *The General Theory*. This type of model building has been launched independently of Keynes by Frisch, Tinbergen and Lundberg. But nobody would deny that many others, who later became active in that field, thought they were merely dynamizing Keynes.

12. H. Myint, "The 'Classical Theory' of International Trade and the Underdeveloped Countries," *Economic Journal*, June 1958, pp. 317–337. A. Smith, *Wealth of Nations*, Vol. 1, Cannan ed.,

p. 413. J. S. Mill, *Principles*, Ashley ed., p. 581. Myint distinguishes from the dynamic "productivity" theory, the "vent-of-surplus" theory and distinguishes the latter also from the static comparative cost theory. This distinction I find unconvincing. The "vent-of-surplus" (if it is not part and parcel of the productivity theory) seems to me simply an extreme case of difference in comparative cost—a country exporting things for which it has no use. This case does not call, it seems to me, for a special theory. But Myint is, of course, quite right that if this extreme situation exists (in modern parlance it might be described as disguised unemployment in export industries) it makes trade appear doubly productive and desirable.

13. I am not speaking here of policies concerning international trade such as the imposition of import restrictions. Changes resulting from trade policy measures are trade induced and not autonomous changes.

14. This includes autonomously shifting.

15. In the neo-classical theory they have been somewhat neglected. The reason is perhaps that these factors do not lend themselves well to precise mathematical treatment.

16. This statement is made on the authority of Prof. John Jewkes of Oxford who has made a close study of sixty major industrial innovations (in the Schumpeterian sense) and comes to the following conclusion: "The cases taken as a whole reveal that no country has a monopoly of inventive power. The outstanding names and groups are widely spread over many industrial countries. One significant exception is that in none of sixty cases studied had contributions been made by Russian workers subsequent to the Revolution. Before that date numerous names of distinguished Russian contributors crop up." J. Jewkes, "The Sources of Invention," Lloyd's Bank Review, Jan. 1958, p. 23. The book that contains the material on which the quoted article is based was published under the same title by Macmillan, London, 1958. Note that what I say is that no industrial innovations have come from Russia to the West. That does not mean there are not any. Obviously, in the field of military technology they are doing quite well and it would be surprising if they had not made any innovations elsewhere. But they are

probably minor compared with Western achievements and at any rate none has come out.

17. *Principles of Political Economy.*
18. G. Myrdal in his Cairo lectures and elsewhere criticizes classical theory for teaching that free trade will equalize living standards internationally, while according to him, the opposite is the case. Myrdal's own views will be critically examined in the text.
19. With respect to the chances of the less developed countries to catch up with the advanced countries the old classical writers were too optimistic, because of their belief that, owing to the inexorable law of diminishing returns, there was an upper limit in the level of economic development which no country could ever pierce. Few economists would deny nowadays that the progress of science and technology may well stave off the dismal consequences of the law of diminishing returns indefinitely or at least for a long time to come.
20. *Manifesto of the Communist Party* by Karl Marx and Friedrich Engels. Authorized English Translation, International Publishers, New York, 1932. See especially pages 11–14.
21. As a typical example of a staunch Marxist, let me quote an American, Paul Sweezy. In a paper "Marxism: A Talk to Students," (*Monthly Review*, New York, Oct. 1958) he admits that Marx was wrong in believing that workers in the advanced countries would get poorer all the time. Workers there have "a tolerable even if degraded (!) life." But the advanced countries "increasingly (!) impose the burdens on the peoples of the colonies and the raw material producing countries." (p. 221).
22. Myrdal, Cairo Lectures, p. 29.
23. Myrdal, *An International Economy*, p. 2.
24. The most important studies are C. P. Kindleberger's monumental book, *The Terms of Trade: A European Case Study* (New York, 1956); P. T. Ellsworth's, "The Terms of Trade between Primary Producing and Industrial Countries, *Inter American Economic Affairs*, Summer 1956; T. Morgan's "The Long-Run Terms of Trade between Agriculture and Manufacturing," *Econometrica*, April 1957, p. 360. I myself have tried to sum up the case in a paper "The Terms of Trade

and Economic Development," Round Table of International Economic Association, Rio de Janeiro August 1957. This paper will be published in the proceedings of that conference by Macmillan, London. A German translation has appeared in the *Zeitschrift fur Nationalokonomie*, Vienna, Austria 1958. Another briefer summary of the discussions will be found in the excellent paper by G. M. Meier, "International Trade and International Inequality," in *Oxford Economic Papers*, October 1958.

25. See especially U.N. Economic Commission for Latin America, *The Development of Latin America and its Principle Problems*, New York, 1950. The original statistical basis is contained in the U.N. report *Relative Prices of Exports and Imports of Underdeveloped Countries*, New York, 1949. Myrdal makes reservations concerning the findings of these reports, but he accepts the Singer-Prebisch thesis nonetheless. See *The International Economy*, p. 231–2.

26. "Convertibility and Triangular Trade," *Economic Journal*, Sept. 1955.

27. Care must also be taken when making long run comparison to place base year and given year at the same cycle phase.

28. W. Stanley Jevons in his gloomy book *The Coal Question: An Inquiry Concerning the Progress of the Nation, and the Probable Exhaustion of the Coal Mines*, (1st ed., London, 1865; 3rd ed. revised, edited by A. W. Flux, London, 1906.) took up the theme. (See chapter XIII of the 3rd edition.) I have already mentioned that these British views were strongly echoed in Germany around the turn of the century.

29. "The Changing Structure of the British Economy," *Economic Journal*, Sept. 1954)

30. Since what matters for welfare purposes is the single factoral terms of trade, it is well to remember that, unlike the commodity terms of trade (or the double factoral terms of trade) the single factoral terms of trade may improve (or deteriorate) for two trading countries (or groups of countries) at the same time. Suppose, for example, the commodity terms of trade have remained unchanged, but each of two trading countries has been able to reduce the cost of its export products. Then each gets more commodities per unit of productive resources exported.

This is what usually happens in a developing world.

31. See Dr. Kostner's "Comments on Professor Nurkse's capital Accumulation in Underdeveloped Countries." (*L'Egypte Contemporaine*, No. 272, 1952) and his "Marginal Comments on the Problem of Underdeveloped Countries." (*Wirtschaftsdienst*, Hamburg, Germany, May 1954.) Viner, "Some Reflections on — the concept of Disguised Unemployment, in *"Contribuscoes Analise do Desenvolvimento Economico."* Essays in honor of Eugenio Gudin, Rio de Janeiro, 1957. T. W. Schultz, "The Role of Government in Promoting Economic Growth," in L. D. White, ed., *The State of the Social Sciences* (Chicago, Ill., 1956) and *The Economic Text in Latin America*, New York State School of Industrial and Labor Relations, Cornell University Bulletin 35, 1956. Professor E. Gudin has told the writers many times that what underdeveloped countries are suffering from is not disguised unemployment, but low levels of productivity not only of manual labor, but managerial labor, engineering labor and so on. This, I believe, hits the nail on the head.

32. "Prospects for an International Economy," *World Politics*, April 1957, p. 466.

33. See the former of the publications mentioned, p. 375.

34. The second publication mentioned above, pp. 1–15. See also the previously cited article by G. M. Meier, who quotes Schultz and other sources.

35. Professor Nurkse was, of course, always aware of the fact that the cure for disguised unemployment was not that easy.

36. New Haven, U.S.A., 1958. I hope Professor Hirschman will accept my saying that he developed brilliantly an idea which the "old-fashioned" economist might have evolved, as a compliment, as in fact it is meant.

37. Myrdal, *Economic Theory and Underdeveloped Regions* (London, 1957, p. 23.) This is a revised version of the author's Cairo lectures.

38. Every economist knows (or should know) that static equilibrium analysis has to be taken *cum grano salis*. After a change equilibrium must be thought of to be established not instantaneously, but usually through a dynamic process, possibly after some oscillations.

39. Modern growth theorists have elaborated on this well-known theme with great aplomb and much display of a pretentious terminology, "vicious circle of poverty," "minimum speed for successful take-off into sustained growth," and similar metaphors, which add little to our understanding.

40. Professor Hirschman (*op. cit.* and in *American Economic Review*, Sept. 19, 1957, pp. 559–570) speaks of "trickling down" and "polarization effects" instead of "spreading" and "backsetting." As compared with Myrdal, his perspective is broader, his treatment of the problem better balanced and his conclusions less dismal and pessimistic for the less developed countries.

41. The United States and other overseas countries have, of course, benefited tremendously from the immigration of skilled workers, engineers, scientists and so on from the Old World—the last big wave having been set in motion by Nazi and communist oppression. Some damage has undoubtedly been done, by this migration, to the countries of origin, but their economic development has not been seriously held up.

42. But even as far as the relations between regions of one country are concerned, two things ought to be remembered; the movement of labor and capital between the two regions is obviously in the interest of the resources that do more (although it damages the complementary factors of production, human as well as material, that are left behind in the stagnant region), and secondly, it is difficult to see how this whole movement could happen if conditions for development in the South were not less favorable than in the North. Hence the movement North may well be in the interest of the country as a whole.

43. The expert will recognize this as the Graham case or the typical infant industry situation. Lack of reference to the relevant theoretical concepts and literature makes it, however, difficult to pin down Myrdal's strictures. I try to give it the most reasonable interpretation possible.

Pioneer Lecture

1. Gunnar Myrdal, *Development and Underdevelopment*, 50th Anniversary Commemoration Lectures (Cairo: National Bank

of Egypt, 1959), p. 29.

2. Gunnar Myrdal, *An International Economy* (New York, N.Y.: Harper, 1956), p. 2.

3. Alexander Hamilton is also claimed as an early practitioner of industrial policy.

4. See Gerald M. Meier's masterly introduction, "The Formative Period," in *Pioneers in Development*, Gerald M. Meier and Dudley Seers, eds. (New York, N.Y.: Oxford University Press, 1984), p. 5.

5. "Five Stages in My Thinking on Development," in Meier and Seers, *Pioneers in Development*, p. 175.

6. Hourly wage rates, nominal and real, did not change much, but real annual earnings increased sharply because unemployment disappeared and the work week returned to its normal length. The situation changed two or three years later when rearmament hit its full stride and price controls clouded the picture. For details, see Gerhard Bry (assisted by Charlotte Boschan), *Wages in Germany, 1871–1945* (Princeton, N.J.: Princeton University Press, 1960).

The Nazis' economic successes did not go unnoticed in the Third World. Hitler's economic wizard, Hjamar Schacht, who was acquitted by the Nuremberg tribunal of war crimes, was after the war retained as a consultant by some developing countries. Interestingly, his advice proved to be too conservative for the governments that consulted him.

7. This prestige was by no means accorded only by outright fellow travelers and Soviet sympathizers.

8. The title of a famous book by Axel Leijonhufvud, *On Keynesian Economics and the Economics of Keynes: A Study of Monetary Theory* (New York, N.Y.: Oxford University Press, 1968). See also T. W. Hutchison, *Keynes Versus the Keynesians. . .?* Hobart Papaerback no. 11 (London, England: Institute of Economic Affairs, 1977).

Although Keynes himself changed his views after the publication of the *General Theory*, not many of his followers could keep pace with the quick turns of the master.

9. See "The Decade of the Twenties," *American Economic Review Supplement* (May 1946), reprinted in *Essays of J. A. Schumpeter*,

Richard V. Clemence, ed. (Cambridge, Mass.: Addison-Wesley, 1951), p. 214.

10. I discuss the misinterpretations of the Great Depression further in *The Problem of Stagflation: Reflections on the Microfoundation of Macroeconomic Theory and Policy* (Washington, D.C.: American Enterprise Institute, 1985); also to appear in *Political Business Cycles and the Political Economy of Stagflation*, Thomas D. Willet, ed. (San Francisco, Calif.: Pacific Institute for Public Policy, forthcoming).

11. We have become familiar with stagflation, the vicious form of an inflationary recession. And the possibility of an inflationary depression cannot be entirely excluded. I have given reasons why I think that this is unlikely in "The Great Depression: Can it Happen Again? in *The Business Cycle and Public Policy, 1920–80*, a compendium of papers submitted to the Joint Economic Committee of the U.S. Congress, November 28, 1980; reprinted as AE1 Reprint no. 18 (Washington, D.C.: American Enterprise Institute, January 1981).

12. *Yale Review* (Summer 1933), pp. 755, 758.

13. Quoted in R. F. Harrod, *The Life of John Maynard Keynes* (New York, N.Y.: Harcourt Brace, 1951), pp. 567–68.

14. Ibid.

15. Lionel (Lord) Robbins, *Autobiography of an Economist* (London, England and New York, N.Y.: Macmillan, 1971), p. 156.

16. See Nicholas (Lord) Kaldor, "The Nemesis of Free Trade" (1977), reprinted in his *Further Essays in Applied Economics* (New York, N.Y.: Holmes and Meier, 1978), and *The Economic Consequences of Mrs. Thatcher: Speeches in the House of Lords 1979–1982* (London, England: Duckworth, 1983).

17. But there can be no doubt that it is very bad advice for the developed countries, too. Kaldor does not make it clear whether he assumes internal or external economies to be the reason for increasing returns. He does not even mention this vital distinction. With regard to internal economies, the enormous advance of transportation, communications, and information technology has progressively undermined the strength of local monopolies, enhanced the importance of large free trade areas, and made protectionist policies increasingly more costly and

obsolete. External economies are attached not merely to manufacturing industries; service industries are equally important.

18. Agricultural protection was politically motivated to help the
Junkers (large estate-owners in Germany); see Alexander
Gerschenkron, *Bread and Democracy in Germany* (Berkeley,
Calif.: University of California Press, 1943). The protection of
the steel industry enabled the German steel cartel to dump
steel at low prices abroad. This was helpful for steel-using
manufacturing industries, especially in the free trade countries, Great Britain and the Netherlands, but was resented by
the German manufacturing industries.

19. See John Maynard Keynes, "The Balance of Payments in the
United States," *Economic Journal*, vol. 56, no. 222 (1946), p.
186.

20. See *The Collected Writings of John Maynard Keynes*, Donald
Moggridge, ed. (London, England: Macmillan and Cambridge
University Press, 1980), vol. 26, for the extensive exchange of
letters and views. Unfortunately, Prebisch never returned to
his early liberal beliefs as far as I know.

21. See my paper, "Critical Observations on Some Current Notions
in the theory of Economic Development," *Industria*, no. 2
(Bologna, Italy: Societa Editrice Il Mulino, 1957).

22. The irony is heightened by the fact that Prebisch had been fully
aware of the mismanagement.

23. "The Terms of Trade Controversy and the Evolution of Soft
Financing: Early Years in the U.N.", in Meier and Seers,
Pioneers in Development; and "Ideas and Policy: The Sources of
UNCTAD," *IDS Bulletin*, vol. 15, no. 3 (July 1984), pp. 14–17.

24. "Critical Observations." See also my "Terms of Trade and
Economic Development," in *Economic Development for Latin
America: Proceedings of a Conference Held by the International
Economic Association*, Howard S. Ellis, ed., assisted by Henry
C. Wallich (London, England: Macmillan, 1961); and "The
Liberal International Economic Order in Historical Perspec-
tive," in *Challenges to a Liberal International Economic Order*,
Ryan C. Amacher and others, eds. (Washington, D.C.: Ameri-
can Enterprise Institute, 1979). My views on the terms of trade
were foreshadowed in or based on what I said more than fifty

years ago in *The Theory of International Trade*, 1st German ed. 1933, rev. English ed. 1936.

25. Princeton, N.J.: Princeton University Press for the NBER, 1963; the quotation that follows in the text is from p. 76. The coverage of Lipsey's volume is more comprehensive than the title suggests. The book also contains price, quantity, and terms of trade indexes for the United Kingdom and continental industrial Europe, which come mainly from C.P. Kindleberger, *The Terms of Trade: A European Case Study* (New York, N.Y.: St. Martin's, 1984), pp. 415–45, which confirms and strengthens Lipsey's conclusions.

26. On the policy conclusions, see also Bela Balassa, "Comment," in Meier and Seers, *Pioneers in Development*, pp. 304–11.

27. 1st ed., London 1865; see especially chap. 13 of the 3rd ed., A. W. Flux, ed. (London, 1906). Keynes related that Jevons had the courage of his convictions. He "laid in such large stores not only of writing-paper, but also of thick brown packing paper, that even today (1936), more than fifty years after his death, his children have not used up the stock he left behind him of the latter; though his purchases seem to have been more in the nature of a speculation than for his personal use, since his own notes were mostly written on the backs of old envelopes and odd scraps, of which the proper place was the waste-paper basket." Keynes's *Essays in Biography*, new edition, with three additional essays edited by Geoffrey Keynes (New York, N.Y.: Horizon Press, 1951), p. 266.

28. "The Changing Sturcture of the British Economy," *Economic Journal* (September 1954).

29. There exists an extensive literature on the terms of trade. A large part was reviewed by T. Morgan, "Trends in Terms of Trade and Their Repercussions on Primary Producers," in *International Trade Theory in a Developing World*, Roy Harrod, ed. (London, England: International Economic Association, 1963), pp. 52–95. See also his "The Long-Run Terms of Trade Between Agriculture and Manufacturing," *Econometrica* (1967); Kindleberger, *The Terms of Trade*; and P. T. Ellsworth, "The Terms of Trade between Primary Producing and Industrial countries," *Inter-American Affairs* (Summer

1956). There is no support for the Prebisch-Singer hypothesis in any of these works.

30. "Critical Observations."

31. Ibid.

32. Washington, D.C.: Brookings Institution, 1967, pp. 70–71. See also Arnold C. Harberger and David Wall, "Harry G. Johnson as a Development Economists," *Journal of Political Economy*, vol. 92, no. 4 (August 1984), p. 623.

33. J. R. Hicks, "The Long-Run Dollar Problems: Inaugural Lecture," *Oxford Economic Papers* (June 1953); and D. H. Robertson, *Britain in the World Economy* (London, England: Allen and Unwin, 1954). For further references, see P. T. Bauer and A. A. Walters, "The State of Economics," *Journal of Law and Economics*, vol. 18, no. 1 (April 1975), p. 5; and Gottfried Haberler, "Dollar Shortage?" in *Foreign Economic Policy for the United States*, Syemour Harris, ed. (New York, N.Y.: Greenwood Press, 1948), p. 42.

In the 1920s J. M. Keynes argued in his famous dispute with Bertil Ohlin that Germany would not be able to pay reparations because demand for German exports abroad was inelastic. It is now generally agreed that Ohlin was right and Keynes's elasticity pessimism was wrong. Alfred Marshall had also emphatically rejected the idea of inelastic demand for a country's exports.

34. The list of publications and country studies in which the theory has been developed is impressive. I mention a few: Hollis Chenery with Irma Adelman "Foreign Aid and Economic Development: The Case of Greece," *Review of Economics and Statistics*, no. 48 (February 1966); Hollis Chenery with A. Strout, "Foreign Assistance and Economic Development," *American Economic Review*, no. 56 (September 1966); and Hollis Chenery and Moises Syrquin, *Patterns of Development, 1950–1970* (London, England: Oxford University Press, 1975). Especially useful is Henry Bruton, "The Two-Gap Approach to Aid and Development," *American Economic Review*, no. 56 (September 1966), and the reply by Chenery, "The Two Gap Approach to Aid and Development: A Reply to Bruton," in the same issue of *American Economic Review*. The theory has been

sharply criticized by Deepak Lal in *The Poverty of "Development Economics,"* Hobart Paperback no. 16 (London, England: Institute of Economic Affairs, 1983).

35. I myself share the general view that on the whole the Marshall Plan was a very constructive and beneficial policy, even though the advice of the American administrators of the plan to the recipients of aid was not always the best.

36. I discussed the infant industry protection in *The Theory of International Trade.*

37. See Albert Hirschman's essay in *The Theory and Experience of Economic Development: Essays in Honor of Sir W. Arthur Lewis,* Mark Gersovitz, Carlos F. Diaz-Alejandro, Gustav Ranis, and Mark R. Rosenweig, eds. (London, England: Allen and Unwin, 1982); and Hans Singer, "Ideas and Policy: The Sources of UNCTAD."

38. Similar views were expressed in Germany by conservative economists such as Albert Hahn and Wilhelm Ropke. They spoke of "secondary deflation," which enormously aggravated the cyclical decline caused by "structural maladjustments." The secondary depression required strong expansionary measures, including government deficit spending.

39. Milton Friedman, in "The Monetary Theory of Henry Simons," *Journal of Law and Economics,* vol. 10 (October 1967), p. 7, writes "There is clearly great similarity between the views expressed by Simons and by Keynes—as to the causes of the Great Depression, the impotence of monetary policy, and the need to rely extensively on fiscal policy. Both men placed great emphasis on the state of business expectations and assigned a critical role to the desire for liquidity [on the] 'absolute' liquidity preference under conditions of deep depression . . . It was this that meant that changes in the quantity of money produced by the monetary authorities would simply be reflected in opposite movements in velocity and have no effect on income or employment." See also Herbert Stein, *The Fiscal Revolution in the United States* (Chicago, Ill.: University of Chicago Press, 1969), and "Early Memories of a Keynes I Never Met," *AEI Economist* (Washington, D.C.: American Enterprise Institute, June 1983); and J. Ronnie Davis, *The New Economics*

and the Old Economists (Ames, Iowa: Iowa State University Press, 1971).

40. See Haberler, "Critical Observations," p. 3.
41. Rosenstein-Rodan in a famous article refers to East European countries. His figures have been critically analyzed and found wanting by Berdj Kenadjian, "Disguised Unemployment in Underdeveloped Countries," *Zeitschrift fur Nationalokonomie*, vol. 21 (1961), pp. 216–23, part of a Ph.D. dissertation, Harvard University, 1962.
42. In my 1957 article, "Critical Observations," I pointed out that the argument has been used to advocate protection for industry so that inefficient labor can be drawn from agriculture and educated on the job in industry. This is, of course, the infant industry argument for protection. The scope and limits of the argument have been thoroughly discussed in the classical and neoclassical literature by John Stuart Mill, Alfred Marshall, Frank W. Taussig, and others.
43. In *Contribuicoes a Analise do Desenvolvimento Economico* (Rio de Janeiro, Brazil: Livraria Agir Editora, 1957), pp. 346–49.
44. *Transforming Traditional Agriculture* (New York, N.Y.: Arno Press, 1976), p. 70.
45. *Internationational Trade and Economic Development*, 50th Anniversary Commemoration Lectures (Cairo, Egypt: National Bank of Egypt, 1959). See also my paper, "An Assessment of the Current Relevance of the Theory of Comparative Advantage in Agricultural Production and Trade," *International Journal of Agrarian Affairs*, vol. 4, no. 3 (May 1964). Both papers are reprinted in *Economics of Trade and Development*, James D. Theberge, ed. (New York, N.Y.: Wiley, 1968).
46. See John Stuart Mill, *Principles of Political Economy*, Ashley edition (London, England: Longmans, Green, 1909), Bk. 3, chap. 17, sec. 5, pp. 581–82. On Mill's theory see Hla Myint, "The 'Classical Theory' of International Trade and the Under Developed Countries," *Economic Journal* (June 1958), pp. 317–37; reprinted in Theberge's *Economics of Trade and Development*.
47. See, for example, *The Economic Development of Latin American and Its Principal Problems* (New York, N.Y.: ECLA, 1950).

The theory was endorsed by Nicholas Kaldor; see his "Stabilizing the Terms of Trade of Underdevelped Countries," paper submitted to the Rio de Janeiro Conference organized by Yale University, January 1963.

48. *Wall Street Journal*, December 26, 1984.
49. Ashley edition, p. 922. Mill was fully aware of the great danger, not to say certainty, that in practice infant industry protection will be carried from "infancy to senility," to quote Bauer again.
50. See Rosenstein-Rodan's contributuion to Meier and Seers, *Pioneers in Development*, pp 209–14, summarizing and updating the conclusion of his well-known article, "Problems of Industrialization of Eastern and South-Eastern Europe," *Economic Journal*, vol. 53 (June-September 1943), pp. 202–11.
51. Gary Becker, *Human Capital*, 2nd ed. (Cambridge, Mass.: National Bureau of Economic Research, 1975), pp. 19–20, 26–28.
52. This section is based on my paper, "An Assessment of the Current Relevance of the Theory of Comparative Advantage to Agricultural Production and Trade," *International Journal of Agrarian Affairs*, vol. 4, no. 3 (May 1964).
53. Tibor Scitovsky, "Two Concepts of External Economies," *Journal of Political Economy* (April 1954); reprinted in *The Economics of Underdevelopment: A Series of Articles and Papers*, A. N. Agarwala and P. Singh, eds. (London, England: Oxford University Press, 1963), p. 305.
54. Ibid, pp. 305–6.
55. Ibid, p. 304.
56. *The Poverty of "Development Economics,"* p. 106.
57. Since this was written, the *Economist* (May 18, 1985, p. 73) has taken up the subject. It points out that "many developing countries are still letting their exchange rates become overvalued. The results are always bad, sometimes disastrous." In other words, many developing countries use controls to prop up the exchange rate.
58. Richard T. Ely Lecture, *American Economic Review*, vol. 67 (February 1977), p. 14 (emphasis added). Kuznets's findings about growth in the developing countries are reported at some length in his *Economic Growth of Nations: Total Output and*

Production Structure (Cambridge, Mass.: Harvard University Press, 1971), chap. 1, and in "Aspects of Post-World War II Growth in Less Developed Countries," in *Evolution, Welfare, and Time in Economics: Essays in Honor of Nicholas Georgescu-Roegen*, A. M. Tang, E. M. Westfield, and James E. Worley, eds. (Lexington, Mass.: Lexington Books, 1976), chap. 3. Kuznets's findings have been confirmed in an important paper by Irving Kravis and Robert Lipsey, "The Diffusion of Economic Growth in the World Economy, 1950–1980," in *International Comparisons of Productivity and Causes of the Slow-down*, John Kendrick, ed. (Washington, D.C.: American Enterprise Institute, 1984), pp. 109–52; they use later data for 1950–80, which has become available since Kuznets wrote.

59. Kuznets, "Aspects of Post-World War II Growth," p. 40.
60. Ibid, pp. 40–41.

Comment
W. Max Corden

1. For a fuller survey, see Robert E. Baldwin, "Gottfried Haberler's Contributions to International Trade Theory and Policy," *Quarterly Journal of Economics*, vol. 97, no. 1 (February 1982), pp. 141-48.
2. *Economic Journal* (June 1950).
3. First ed., Geneva: League of Nations, 1937; 5th ed. (Cambridge, Mass.: Harvard University Press, 1964).
4. "Critical Notes on Rational Expectations," *Journal of Money, Credit and Banking*, vol. 12, no. 4, pt. 2 (November 1980) pp. 833–36.
5. Princeton, N.J.: International Finance Section, Princeton University, 1955.
6. *Industry and Trade in Some Developing Countries: A Comparative Study* (London, England: Oxford University Press, 1970).

Comment
Ronald Findlay

1. Marice Dobb, *An Essay on Economic Growth and Planning* (London, England: Routledge and Kegan Paul, 1960); A. K. Sen, *Choice of Techniques* (London, England: Blackwell, 1960).
2. "Alternative Patterns of Growth under Conditions of Stagnant Export Earnings," *Oxford Economic Papers* (February 1961).
3. "Static Models and Current Problems in International Economics," *Oxford Economic Papers* (June 1949).
4. Gottfried Haberler, "Some Problems in the Pure Theory of International Trade," *Economic Journal* (June 1950).
5. J. N. Bhagwati and V. K. Ramaswami, "Domestic Distortions, Tariffs, and the Theory of Optimum Subsidy, " *Journal of Political Economy*, vol. 71 (February 1963); and Robert E. Baldwin, "Gottfried Haberler's Contributions to International Trade Theory and Policy," *Quarterly Journal of Economics*, vol. 97, no. 1 (February 1982).
6. Princeton, N. J.: International Finance Section, Princeton University, 1955.
7. "Patterns of Trade and Investment in a Dynamic Model of International Trade," *Review of Economic Studies* (January 1965).
8. Ronald Findlay, *International Trade and Development Theory* (New York, N.Y.: Columbia University Press, 1973).
9. Ronald Findlay, "An 'Austrian' Model of International Trade and Interest Rate Equalization," *Journal of Political Economy* (December 1978).
10. Ronald Findlay and Henryk Kierzkowski, "International Trade and Human Capital," *Journal of Political Economy* (December 1983).
11. *Manual of Industrial Product Analysis in Developing Countries* (Paris, France: Organization for Economic Co-operation and Development, 1969).
12. See Ronald Findlay and Stanislaw Wellisz, "Project Evaluations, Shadow Prices and Trade Policy," *Journal of Political Economy* (June 1976); and T. N. Srinivasan and J. N. Bhagwati, "Shadow Prices for Project Selection in the Presence of

Distortions," *Journal of Political Economy* (February 1978).

13. "Economic Implications of Learning by Doing," *Review of Economic Studies*, vol. 29 (1962), pp. 155–73.

14. *Economic Growth, Development and Foreign Trade* (New York, N.Y.: Wiley, 1970).

15. See H. G. Johnson, "Optimal Trade Intervention in the Presence of Domestic Distortions, in *Trade, Growth and Balance of Payments*, R. E. Baldwin and others, eds. (Chicago, Ill.: Rand McNally; Amsterdam: North-Holland, 1965).

16. Paul Streeten, "A Cool Look at Outward-Looking Strategies for Development," *World Economy* (September 1982); and Ronald Findlay, "Comment" on A. O. Krueger, "Export-Led Industrial Growth Reconsidered," in *Trade and Growth of the Advanced Developing Countries of the Pacific Basin*, W. Hong and L. B. Krause, eds. (Seoul, Korea: Korea Development Institute, 1981).

17. "The Infant Export Industry Argument," *Canadian Journal of Economics* (May 1984).

18. J. R. Hicks, "The Long-Run Dollar Problem," *Oxford Economic Papers* (June 1953); H. G. Johnson, "Economic Expansion and International Trade," *Manchester School of Economic and Social Studies* (May 1955).

19. Examples are Edmar L. Bacha, "An Interpretation of Unequal Exchange from Prebisch-Singer to Emmanuel," *Journal of Development Economics*, vol. 5 (1978), pp. 319–30; Lance Taylor, *Structuralist Macroeconomics: Applicable Models for the Third World* (New York, N.Y.: Basic Books, 1983); and Ronald Findlay, "The Terms of Trade and Equilibrium Growth in the World Economy," *American Economic Review* (June 1980).

20. W. A. Lewis, "Economic Development with Unlimited Supplies of Labor," *Manchester School of Economic and Social Studies* (May 1954); and R. M. Solow, "A Contribution to the Theory of Economic Growth," *Quarterly Journal of Economics* (February 1956).

21. Arghiri Emmanuel, *Unequal Exchange: A Study of the Imperialism of Trade* (New York, N.Y.: Monthly Review Press, 1974); and W. A. Lewis, *Aspects of Tropical Trade, 1883–1965*, Wicksell Lectures, 1969.

22. As I have argued in "International Distributive Justice," *Journal of International Economics* (February 1982).